CONTENTS

DEDICATION

This book is dedicated to my father and mother, Clarence and Elva Clouser. They started me on this path at a young age and I still haven't found the end. I thank them for it all. I also have heartfelt thanks to my wife, Joan, for her undying patience with me.

FOREWORD

Bob Clouser is many things, but aside from being a wonderful human being, Bob is an excellent fly fisherman. Many who write articles and books on the sport are skilled and well-intentioned but lack in-depth experience in fly fishing. Not so with Bob. He has spent decades analyzing, experimenting, and successfully catching fish in fresh and salt water. What you read here is based on solid experience and will help you tie better flies, understand why you do or do not catch fish, and enjoy the sport even more.

The first portion of this book is valuable to anyone who ties or fishes flies. Bob gives so many insights and tips on fly design and how to tie flies correctly, that this section alone makes this book worth buying.

Always an experimenter when conventional fly patterns are not working, Bob tweaks patterns, or even invents new ones, to fool fish. His Clouser Deep Minnow is undoubtedly the most popular fly pattern to be developed in the last several decades. It is used across the planet to catch fish in fresh or salt water. From his decades of fly fishing on the water and many years of guiding, he has developed a number of patterns that meet difficult situations. In this book, Bob supplies information on why and how to fish these flies and includes excellent photos of how to tie each one.

If you are a serious fly fisherman, I believe this book is one of the most useful that has been published in some time.

—Lefty Kreh

ACKNOWLEDGMENTS

I thank Jay Nichols for his untiring help and as the motivator in organizing the text and photographs to complete my first book. This book is a lifetime of effort put forth through the encouragement of many, mainly my family—my wife, Joan; sons, Bob Clouser Jr., David, and Michael; and my two daughters, Sherry and Robin. They all missed a lot of weekend drives due to my fishing and fly tying addiction. I thank Lefty Kreh not only as my buddy but for tutoring and mentoring me for over twenty years. His honesty and integrity in guidance was always and will always be treasured by me. Lefty has made the serious part fun, and I would not have it any other way. He calls me the oldest kid he ever met, and we found out we both still are.

There are many fishing buddies and close friends that are responsible for my career in fly fishing and tying that have given me ideas and the encouragement to write this book. I could list hundreds of names, but I decided my friends are so valuable that I won't name names in case I forget just one. It would not be fair to do so. I think you all know who you are and I sincerely thank you.

—Bob Clouser

INTRODUCTION: DESIGNING FLIES

Part of the fun of fly fishing for me is learning about nature. I enjoy observing the insects, baitfish, and other food items I use as guides to build my flies. But careful observation brings more than enjoyment; it is essential if you want to be an effective angler and fly tier. A quick glance at a picture in a book or a one-time observation will not do. If you want to tie flies that catch more fish—and catch fish consistently—you must study the behaviors, habitats, and physical characteristics of the foods fish eat.

In 1952, my dad bought me a fly-tying kit for my fourteenth birthday. For tools, it contained a simple vise, a spring-loaded bobbin, hackle pliers, and a needle. Some instructions on two sheets of paper explained how to make flies from the assortment of hooks and patches of fur, loose feathers, and threads and yarns of various colors. I taught myself slowly how to use the tools and materials and made all types of concoctions.

My dad saw that I was interested in fly tying, so in 1954, he purchased *Family Circle's Guide to Trout Flies and How to Tie Them* by Raymond Camp. It was loaded with full-color pictures of flies and listed their ingredients.

My approach to fly design most often begins and ends onstream, with a lot of time in between at the bench. A pattern has to cast well, look good in the water, and catch fish for me to consider it a keeper. Mike O'Brien casts to a Susquehanna bridge pier.
BOB CLOUSER PHOTO

That fly-tying guide had paintings in it instead of photographs, and for the life of me, I could not figure out the actual colors of the materials or the flies. The colors weren't true to life; there was a big difference between the rich reds and browns on the pages and the colors of the actual materials I held in my hands. Instead of copying the real thing—nature—I tried, with frustration, to copy the illustrations.

Today many new tiers face a similar challenge. When a beginner reads a recipe that calls for a brown hackle, he is faced with the tough task of determining which brown is "brown." If you look at the amazing array of genetic hackles available today, no two are exactly alike in color. This can be frustrating. Or if you are sitting down at the bench to imitate a black-nose dace but have never seen one for yourself, you take a leap of faith to tie fur and feathers to a hook according to the recipe, you call it a dace, and then go out and cast it into the water with confidence.

As I spent more time on the river and on the vise, I began to trust my own observations. Instead of working from a recipe or a perceived color in the book, I simply looked at the natural that I wanted to imitate and found a material that would match the color and movement in the water that I desired. My approach to fly design most often begins and ends onstream, with a lot of time in between at the bench.

Your on-the-water observations of both the bait and the fish that feed on it are the key to successful fly tying and fishing. Others' observations often fall short of your situation on your home water. Though I share with you in this book what I have learned, that is no substitute for your own experience. You also must modify and adapt your techniques depending on your quarry and the fishing situation. Use the information here as a beginning guide to designing patterns for the species you fish for. I hope the basic techniques you learn will help you create your own patterns with more confidence.

Once you design flies that look and act like the real thing in the water, you need to make sure they fish well. Good fly patterns should cast easily, not foul, and be durable enough that you don't have to stop fishing to tie on a new fly when the catching is good. At times, you may have to sacrifice a few of these criteria to achieve other characteristics, but whenever you design a pattern that both catches fish and fishes well, you have a winning fly.

Throughout this book, I provide recipes for fly patterns that have worked well for me and other anglers around the world. These flies are my most successful patterns. Along the way, many of my flies ended up in the trash bin, but these are the survivors. The directions are given for a right-hand tier.

PART I

Tying Clouser Flies

CHAPTER 1

Materials

In this chapter, I describe some of my favorite materials and give tips on handling and selecting them, but I encourage you to explore other materials not mentioned here and make the flies you tie your own creations. Many of the patterns in this book, especially the Clouser Minnow series, are styles of tying rather than specific flies, so you can use a variety of materials in them besides the ones listed here.

HOOKS

The hook is the most important part of the fly. Not only is it what catches the fish, but as a platform on which the fly is tied, it becomes an integral part of a fly's design. Whether for small dry flies or large streamers, hook color, weight, and length all affect the appearance of the fly, how it hooks different species of fish, how the fly tied on it casts, and where it rides in the water—on the top, on the bottom, or somewhere in between.

I tie most Deep Minnows and variations on regular shank or 1XL hooks. These hook lengths are generally suitable for most warm- or saltwater species. I make one exception for trout. Because trout often stun or nip their prey before returning to eat it, I use up to 4XL hooks, and I don't tie the materials off the back of them much longer than one-half of the shank. I try to make sure the hook bend is close to the end of the fly. If you had 4-inch fibers dangling off the back of the hook, you'd most likely miss fish that nip at the fly.

There are many good hooks on the market, and you can tie Clouser Minnows on a variety of them. I like to keep things as simple as possible for my own tying. Here is a list of hook models and their characteristics that I most frequently use for the patterns in this book. You can make substitutions as needed.

I tied many of the freshwater baitfish patterns in this book on the Mustad 3365A, a straight-eye streamer hook with a nickel finish that is not available anymore. The bronze version of the same hook, the Mustad 3366, is a good substitute, as is the Mustad Signature Series S71S SS or the Tiemco 811S.

For saltwater baitfish patterns, I use the Mustad S71S SS. This Signature Series stainless-steel hook is 2X heavy, 1X long, and has a straight eye. The Mustad S74S SS that I use for the Rattle Clouser is a 4X-long-shank version of the S71S SS. I also use the Mustad 34007 and the 39951BLN Demon Circle. The Mustad 34011, the long-shank version of the Mustad 34007, is my choice for the Brightsides Minnows (in both fresh and salt water), the saltwater version of the EZ Popper, and all bendback patterns.

These are the hooks I use for the species I fish for. I also like to use the thinnest-diameter hook possible because thin-diameter hooks penetrate easier than heavy-diameter hooks. But it is important to match the hook to your quarry. For instance, if you are fishing for 100-pound plus tarpon, you may want to experiment with heavier wire hooks; if you are fishing for small panfish or trout and bass, you can more often than not get away with lighter wire hooks.

In each of the pattern descriptions in this book, I provide my recommendations for hooks, but since most of these patterns travel well, you'll surely be fishing these flies for other species that require different hooks. One of the benefits of tying your own flies is that you can use any hook you want. If you are missing fish because the gap is too small, or fine-wire dry-fly hooks are straightening out, or you are not sinking your fly deep enough, take a look at the hook model you're using. Over time, you will develop your own preferences for certain makes

Clousers tied on circle hooks helped us land more tarpon during a two-week trip to the Yucatán Peninsula.
TOM WHITTLE PHOTO

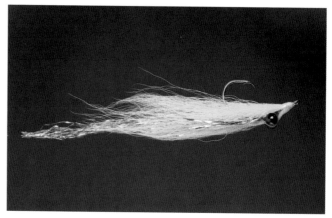

You can easily modify Clouser Minnows to many different styles of hooks, such as circle hooks (shown here), depending on the species you are fishing for.

Bob Clouser getting ready to cast a circle-hook Clouser Deep Minnow to tarpon. TOM WHITTLE PHOTO

and models based on your experience. I list the hook model and size for each fly pattern, but many others will work as well, and you can often substitute similar hooks from other manufacturers.

Circle Hooks

Bait anglers have used circle hooks for a long time, but they have only recently begun to be popular with fly anglers. Both Lefty Kreh and I have had great success tying Deceivers and Deep Minnows on circle hooks. My friend Tom Whittle and I fished with flies tied on circle hooks on a two-week trip to Casa Blanca, Mexico, located on the Yucatán Peninsula on Ascension Bay. We wanted to find out if they would increase the hookup and landing rates for tarpon, a fish species noted for its hook-shaking acrobatics.

These hooks performed better than we expected, but we had to modify our techniques, especially the hook set, when fishing flies tied on them. You cannot set the hook, which is hard for many fly anglers to resist doing. For the circle hook to properly do its job, the fish has to turn away from the angler as soon as it takes the fly. The angler should not do anything until he feels weight moving away. At this point, the hook is in posi-

tion and already set. Using circle hooks, Tom and I found all the tarpon we landed were solidly hooked in the corner of the upper lip, in the tissue between the face and the bony armor-type plate that protects the upper lip.

Circle hooks provide a hooking advantage for other species as well. During our two-week trip, Tom and I hooked fifteen barracuda and landed fourteen of them without wire tippets. We used Rio's 80-pound-test Fluoroflex leader material for bite tippets, and it showed only minor abrasion from the barracuda's teeth from the initial take. The circle-hook flies lodged in the corner of the mouth, making it impossible for the barracuda to bite on the tippet section. Circle hooks worked effectively on bonefish, snook, various species of snapper, and a few jack crevalle. If used properly, we found that these hooks can be a valuable tool in hooking and landing many species of fish. I also enjoyed learning a new and exciting method in the fly-fishing game.

Debarbing Hooks

Before I put a hook in the vise, I often pinch the barb down with a pair of flat needlenose pliers. Though you can pinch barbs down on the water before you fish your flies, debarbing hooks at the bench saves time in the long run and ensures that you don't forget this step when you're on the water thinking about other things.

To debarb a hook, turn it so that the bend is in line with the pliers and the point of the hook faces the tip of the pliers. Insert the hook between the jaws and pinch the barb down. Some people insert the pliers perpendicular to the hook barb and pinch, but this can damage and weaken the hook point.

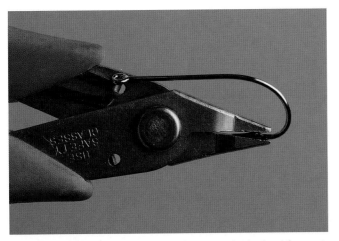

To properly debarb a hook, crimp down on the barb with a pair of flat-faced pliers so that the pliers are in line with the hook point.

Sharpening Hooks

Many hooks come out of the box sharp; others need to be sharpened. There are many ways to sharpen hooks, and everyone has an opinion about the best way. To determine whether a hook is sharp enough, scrape the point against your thumbnail. If the hook hangs up, it's

sharp. Experienced anglers check their hook points frequently when fishing.

To sharpen a hook, insert it into your vise with the point up. Using a fine-grade flat metal file, form a diamond point by making three strokes on the far side of the hook, moving from the barb to the bend, and then repeating that angle on the near side. Try to keep the point as short as possible; long, needle-type points are weak. You can sharpen smaller trout hooks with a diamond-dust fingernail file, available at drugstores.

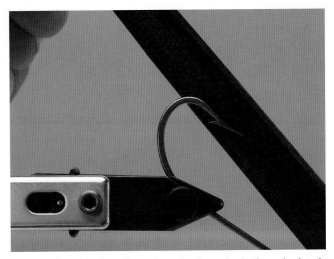

To sharpen a hook, make one stroke from the barb to the bend on the far side of the hook, then repeat on the other side.

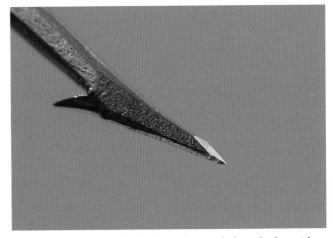

A properly sharpened hook has a diamond-shaped edge with no burrs.

Uni-Thread grips the slippery deer-tail fibers I use in many of my patterns, and it is strong enough that I can use a lot of tension when I tie materials onto the hook. Many tiers tend not to put enough tension on the thread when tying flies. Experiment to determine how

I prefer to keep the spools of thread that I commonly use on bobbins so I don't have to waste time threading one every time I want to change thread color. A tool caddy keeps your tools organized and within reach.

strong your tying thread is, and try to tie at maximum tension for more durable flies.

I also often use Danville fine monofilament-nylon thread. This clear thread is strong, and you can use it in place of regular thread on all of your patterns. Saltwater tiers use a lot of mono thread. Monofilament thread is also available in an extrafine size, but I find it too thin for most applications.

Because monofilament thread is transparent, it won't clash with any colors, so you can use it for all of your flies. The colors of the materials show through the thread wraps, which can add a desirable effect to the fly, especially on epoxy patterns. You need to keep constant tension on the thread when using it, however, or it tends to unwrap. Once the fly is completed, protect the monofilament thread with a coat of epoxy or head cement. I prefer epoxy.

To save time, I keep spools of thread that I use most often on bobbins. I stick the bobbins in a piece of foam or a tool caddy so I can reach them easily. Though not necessary, buying half a dozen bobbins as you begin to develop your collection of fly-tying tools is a worthwhile investment. Down the road, it'll save you time threading bobbins each time you want to change thread color. For those times when you need a bobbin threader, you can whip-finish a loop of monofilament onto a dowel or purchase dental-floss threaders at your local drugstore.

EYES

Once during a conversation about baitfish and their imitations, Lefty Kreh reminded me that a baitfish never stops moving when it's fleeing from a predator. The key

to the success of the Clouser Minnow series of flies is the metallic eyes. The forward weight in the fly causes it to continually dart forward and drop with every pull and pause in the retrieve. This dipping and darting action triggers fish to strike.

Many different sizes, styles, and types of metallic eyes are available from manufacturers, ranging from plain lead that you need to paint, to brass with prismatic eyes in every color imaginable. Well-stocked fly shops carry lead, brass, aluminum, and plastic eyes in different shapes and weights.

When choosing eyes, pay attention to their weight, size, and stem design. For Clouser Minnows, I prefer hourglass- or barbell-shaped eyes with short stems, rather than the older barbell- or dumbbell-shaped eyes with long stems. The hourglass shape centers easily on the hook and does not break as readily as barbell eyes with long stems.

The flies in the Clouser Minnow series are so effective because you can change their weight to fish them at different depths, just like spin fishermen do by changing the size of jig heads in lures. Heavy eyes get the fly down to or near the bottom, and it swims along the bottom on the retrieve rather than at middepth or near the surface. Depending on where the fish are feeding, sometimes a fly with lighter eyes that swims at middepth or near the surface catches more fish.

Small eyes are not just for small hooks. You can add small eyes to large flies when you want a pattern that descends slowly in the water or lands with less splash than a fly with larger eyes. Often a fly that descends slowly—especially if the water is low, clear, and moving slowly—is more effective than a fly that sinks quickly to the bottom. Smallmouth bass, especially, like a slowly descending fly as the currents diminish.

I don't recommend putting large eyes on small hooks. The width of the eye should not exceed the width of the hook gap. If the width of the eye is larger than the hook gap, it reduces the fly's hooking capabilities.

You can also make eyes out of various sizes of metal or plastic bead chain. This allows you to use lightweight eyes for slow-descending flies in shallow, clear water. Many bonefish flies are tied with bead-chain eyes—especially plastic bead chain—because they don't create as much of a disturbance as other metallic eyes when they hit the water. Insert the blades of a pair of wire-cutter side nippers between the beads, making sure both balls extend beyond the jaws, and cut the wire that holds the beads together.

The positioning of weighted eyes on top of the hook causes the fly to ride with the hook up. Often the habitat in which fish are found—especially bass—is lit-

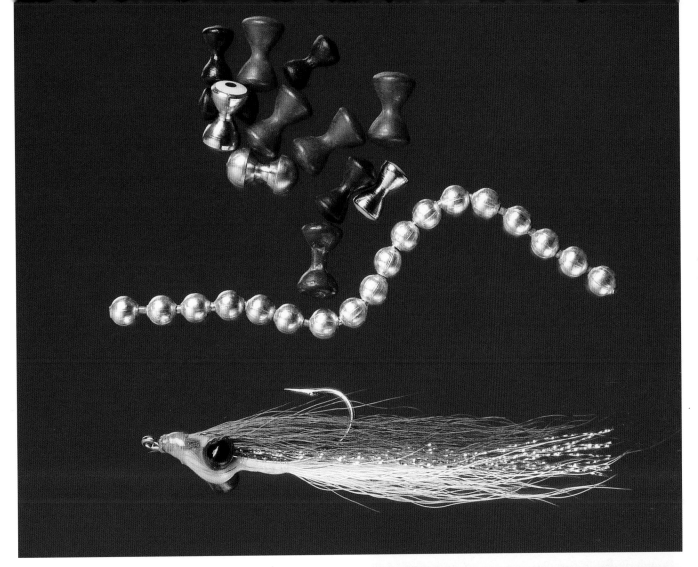

Above: The key to the Clouser Minnow style of tying is the weighted eyes. Eyes come in a variety of shapes and sizes, from bead chain for bonefish to heavy barbell eyes for saltwater patterns. Right: I tie my bonefish flies with a range of eye weights, including metal and plastic beadchain eyes for skinny water and spooky fish.

tered with deadfalls, rocks, and other structure, which catch flies that ride in the water with the hook down. With a Clouser Deep Minnow, you can fish the fly right on the bottom with little fear of damaging the hook point. One of the most common causes of missed strikes is a dull hook, and this happens less frequently with a pattern that rides with the hook up.

I use flat, adhesive-backed prismatic eyes for many of my floating flies, such as EZ Poppers, Floating Minnows, and Crippled Minnows. Adhesive eyes come in different sizes, ranging from $3/32$ to $3/8$ inch in diameter. Most fly shops have a wide selection of diameters and colors to choose from. I use silver and black for most of my flies. To remove an individual eye from the sheet, I use the point of a bodkin.

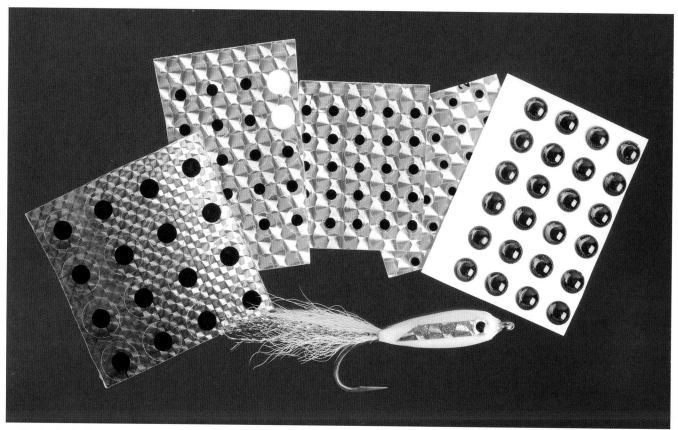

Adhesive-backed prismatic eyes come in a variety of sizes and color combinations. For most of my foam floating flies, such as the Bright Sides Minnow (shown here), I use silver with a black pupil.

Painting the Eyes

Though all-black metallic eyes are effective (especially when coated with a drop of epoxy over each eye), I often paint the plain lead eyes, partly because I like the way they look, and partly because I think a little bit of red triggers fish to strike. Many believe that predators strike at the eyes of their prey, and thus the reason why some fish species have marks resembling eyes on their tails is to trick predators. My favorite color combination is a red eye with a large black pupil. That color combination has never, to my knowledge, deterred strikes. But that doesn't mean those colors work best everywhere. For instance, Tom Earnhardt, an experienced angler in North Carolina, believes false albacore prefer silver eyes with black pupils, and many saltwater tiers are fond of prismatic stick-on eyes in different color combinations, such as red and black, yellow and black, chartreuse and black, and silver and black. Experiment.

You can purchase eyes that are already painted or paint your own. Though you can paint one eye at a time, I use a special holder designed by a friend to paint many eyes at once. It saves time and effort to use such a system. Instead of a jig like mine, you can use alligator clips or bobby pins stuck into a large piece of foam, or slits cut into cardboard to hold the eyes in place while you paint them.

I use lacquer, but you can also use model paint or other methods to color the eyes. To apply the paint, you can use many different tools, such as pieces of wooden dowel, finish nail heads, or watercolor paintbrush handles cut at various lengths. You'll need two different diame-

To paint many eyes at one time, I use a special holder. First I paint the eyes red, and after the red has dried, I paint large black pupils on them.

ters—one for the eye, the other for the pupil. Paint the first color on all the eyes, let them dry, and then paint the pupils a second color. For protection, coat the painted surface with clear fingernail polish such as Sally Hansen Hard as Nails or epoxy for added durability.

GLUES, CEMENTS, AND EPOXIES

Glues, cements, and epoxies all add durability to flies. There are many good products on the market, but for bonding foam popper heads to the hook shank or as a bulletproof substitute for conventional cement applications, I use a waterproof cyanoacrylate glue such as Zap-A-Gap CA+ or Fishin' Glue. Zap-A-Gap is available in various viscosities which are useful for different applications. Zap-A-Gap CA+ is thicker than Zap-A-Gap CA, so it is a better choice for filling the gaps between the two foam bodies used to form heads on the Floating Minnow and Bright Sides Minnow. Zap Gel is even thicker than Zap-A-Gap CA+ and also works well for the foam flies in this book. It comes in a bottle with a brush.

All of these glues dry up in the bottle quickly, and it seems that after only a few days, your new bottle of glue has evaporated or turned to rock, or the cap has become glued shut. To make working with this stuff a bit easier, only cut a small portion of the bottle's tip with scissors or a utility knife. Then poke a small hole in the tip with your bodkin just so that all of the glue doesn't come rushing out at once when you squeeze the bottle. A small drop of this glue goes a long way.

I also like to coat the tip with liquid silicone and wipe it down with a paper towel before putting the cap back on. Silicone slows down the curing process and prevents the glue from sticking to the tip of the bottle; wiping off the glue after each use keeps the cap from sticking. Place a drop of silicone on your fingers, rub them together so that the silicone covers them, and wipe down the nozzle. This method usually works well, although some glues cure right through the silicone.

I usually store my glues in a freezer or a refrigerator if I do not intend to use them for a long period of time. Most fast-drying glues have only a six- to twelve-month life span even if left unopened. These types of glues also can be used as head cement, although many of them do not dry clear or smooth.

When I use head cement as a protective covering, I prefer Wapsi Gloss Coat. It is the most durable head cement I've used. I also often use Sally Hansen Hard as Nails with nylon, which is available in small bottles at most drugstores, or some of the better-quality fly-tying lacquers on the market.

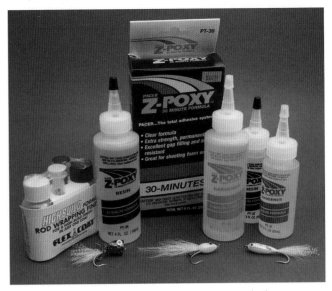

I coat all the heads of my Clouser Minnows with thirty-minute epoxy, such as Z-Poxy. Flex Coat tinted with glitter makes a durable, eye-catching foam popper head on flies such as the EZ Popper, Floating Minnow, and Bright Sides Minnow.

I use epoxy in many fly patterns, either as a head coating or to coat the head and metallic eyes at the same time. Epoxy welds metallic eyes to the hook in the Clouser Minnows, protects and enhances the foam on my EZ Popper and floating minnow imitations, and makes an attractive and durable head coating on any fly for fresh or salt water. For saltwater flies, it is essential. Toothy fish, such as bluefish or barracuda, can make short work of flies without it, and in surf fishing, sand grinds up and destroys fly heads not coated with epoxy.

Epoxy consists of two liquid components: a resin and a hardener. When mixed together in equal parts, the mixture hardens. After you combine the resin and the hardener, you have a working time during which the epoxy can be applied. Once the working time is over, the epoxy sets, becoming a solid. Depending on the epoxy formula (five-minute and thirty-minute are the most popular), the working time can be anywhere from seconds to an hour or longer. Complete curing takes longer than the working time of your epoxy. For instance, five-minute epoxy has a working time of about three minutes and a curing time of ten to fifteen minutes. As a general rule, the longer an epoxy's curing time, the more flexible and resistant to yellowing it is. The most popular brands of five- and thirty-minute epoxies on the market are Devcon, Pacer, and Flex Coat. Other brands may also work, but these three have a proven tying record. I use Pacer thirty-minute Z-Poxy to protect the eyes and heads of most of my flies.

Left: Floating Minnow bodies are marketed as bug bodies. See the chart in chapter 17 to correctly match head size with hook size. Below: Bright Sides Minnow bodies are marketed as ant bodies. Squeeze two together, glue with Zap-A-Gap CA+, and coat with Flex Coat for a quick, durable fly.

Foam cylinders come in many different sizes and colors. Pictured here are $1/4$, $3/8$, and $1/2$ inch. Cut a slit on the bottom of a cylinder and glue it to the hook shank with Zap-A-Gap CA+.

When the clarity and flexibility of the epoxy is more important than the setting time, use a moderate-setting epoxy formula. Thirty-minute epoxy used with a drying wheel provides extended working time for coating the heads of large batches of flies, such as a dozen or more Clouser Minnows or Deceivers, which saves time and materials. As the flies slowly spin on the drying wheel, the epoxy fills all the gaps and covers the thread wraps before it hardens, producing evenly coated heads with smooth surfaces.

I coat my EZ Poppers and the sponge-rubber heads of my Floating Minnows and Bright Sides Minnows with Flex Coat. This rodmaker's epoxy gels in two hours and cures in six. Some types of foam deteriorate when exposed to extreme sunlight, but a fly coated with Flex Coat can last all summer. A light coating with this type of epoxy seals poppers and other floating flies from moisture, enhances their looks, and protects eyes and painted finishes. For glossy fly heads, especially foam poppers, mix a batch of Flex Coat, coat a number of heads at one time, and rotate them on a drying wheel overnight. Apply two coats for best results.

Mix the epoxy on a Post-it Note or some other material you know won't bleed its color into the epoxy. You can add flash to your flies (or bring life to an old one) by adding extrafine glitter to the mixture. Craft stores generally carry a wide assortment of glitter. Pearl glitter is the most popular. Don't add too much glitter, or you'll weaken the bond of the epoxy and it won't cure properly. Once the epoxy is mixed well, apply it to the fly. If you are using a bodkin, rub the epoxy onto the fly with the side of the needle instead of the point. I use a thin metal rod that has no sharp edges from a Griffin bobbin-cleaning kit. Put epoxy only on the thread-covered sections of the fly, unless you have a reason to do otherwise. Try not to get it on the other materials; epoxy cannot be removed from deer-tail fibers or feathers.

Work in a well-ventilated room, following the manufacturer's instructions. Keep paper towels handy to remove liquid epoxy from your tools. Use lacquer thinner to remove hardened epoxy from your applicator, or crack it with a pair of pliers and scrape it off. You can wash sticky resin or hardener off your hands with soap and water, but if you accidentally get the mixed epoxy on your skin, clean the area immediately with isopropyl alcohol. Citrus hand cleaners will remove both liquid and cured epoxy from your skin.

FOAM CYLINDERS, HEADS, AND BODIES

As soon as I discovered foam for fly tying, I pretty much stopped fishing deer-hair patterns when I guided for smallmouth bass. The patterns took me too long to tie. I could tie foam poppers and Crippled Minnows three times faster than trimmed deer-hair patterns, and they were more durable and just as effective.

I use three different types of foam products for the heads and bodies of my floating flies: foam cylinders ranging from 1/4 to 1 inch in diameter for EZ Poppers, sponge rubber bug bodies for Floating Minnows, and sponge rubber ant bodies for Bright Sides Minnows. Foam cylinders and sponge rubber bodies come in a variety of colors.

DEER-TAIL HAIR

Often referred to as bucktail, deer-tail hair, from white-tailed bucks and does, is a versatile and effective fly-tying material that works very well in the water. I used deer-tail fibers for the wings of my first Deep Minnows back in the 1980s and have yet to find a better substitute for most situations.

To cut the hair from a skin, lift the fibers from the base so that they are perpendicular to the skin. This evens the bundle of fibers, but the ends will still be nice and tapered, making these hairs ideal for streamer-type patterns.

When tying baitfish imitations, I do not even the tips of the deer-tail fibers with a hair stacker or other device. Stacking the hairs aligns the tips perfectly, causing the bundle of hair to look as neat as a paintbrush when tied on the fly. This is not the effect I want. Light penetrates uneven tips better than neatly stacked ones and the fly works better in the water.

To prepare the clump of bucktail before tying it in, first thin out the shorter fibers from the base. Holding the tips in your left hand, pull out any loose or short fibers with your right hand from the base of the clump. Generally, you have to pull only the bottom inch or so of fibers. Next, grab the base fibers with your right hand, and pull the long or stray fibers out of the bundle with your left hand.

Unfortunately, not all the deer tail you work with will be perfect. Often you must be able to work with marginal materials and manipulate the fibers with your hands before tying them onto the fly. It's relatively easy to tie nice-looking flies with grade-A materials, but experienced tiers understand their materials well enough to manipulate poorer ones to make good-looking flies.

One of the marks of a good fly tier is the ability to work with marginal materials; another is the ability to identify the best materials to work with and determine which materials to discard or use on other flies for which they are better suited. This is especially true when work-

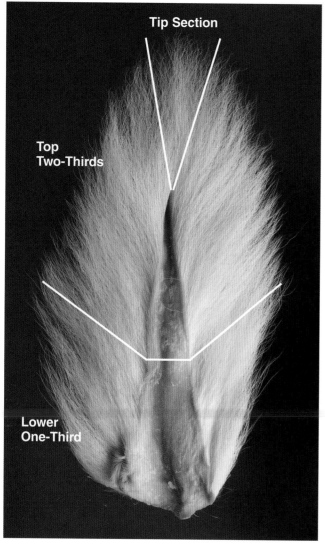

Tip Section

Top
Two-Thirds

Lower
One-Third

Before using the tip section of the deer tail, make sure the tips of the fibers have not been worn flat by the deer. On some deer tails, the tips are usable; on others, they are not.

The top two-thirds is the prime portion of the tail and is where most of the best fibers suited for Clouser Minnows come from.

The lower one-third contains hollow fibers that flare widely when tied onto the hook. You can cut this portion away from the main tail and use it for applications that call for flared deer-hair fibers.

ing with deer tail. Selecting the proper deer tail for the job at hand will help you tie better-looking and better-fishing flies. When tying Clousers or any other type of streamer fly, it's also important that you take the hair from the right part of the deer tail.

To prepare all of my deer tails ahead of time, I generally break off one-quarter of the tail from the bottom and discard it. This bottom portion is the part of the tail

that comes in contact with the rump of the deer. The hair fibers here are hollow, coarse, wide, and often uneven—the wrong characteristics for tying Deep Minnows. If you tie a bunch of these fibers onto a hook shank, they flare. I generally throw this portion away because tails that have been prepared are much easier to store, and I don't have a need for this type of hair.

The tip of the tail has solid fibers. These, together with fibers down about two-thirds the length of the tail, are the best ones for tying Clouser Minnows and other streamer patterns. When you tie fibers from the middle of the tail onto the hook, they do not flare very much. Fibers from the tip flare the least, but they are often shorter. When tying your flies, try to think about the hair you have and the flies you will be tying. The key is to use the longest, straightest fibers for your longer flies and the shorter fibers for your short flies. If possible, don't use the long hair for shorter flies; save this prime hair for when you really need it.

You learn about materials by using them. Once you have worked with a number of deer tails, you'll be able to quickly distinguish between good and bad ones. Before you purchase a deer tail in a fly shop, take it out of the package and inspect it. Fibers that are soft to the touch and not coarse are fine to use; crinkled fibers are a good choice also. Another test is to look at the number of fibers in a bundle the size of one you would use to tie a fly. If the hair tips are fairly even and the clump does not contain a lot of short or long fibers, it will make a good fly.

CALF TAIL

Also called kip tail, calf tail is often used for wings for steelhead and Atlantic salmon flies, as well as for Lee Wulff's popular Wulff series of flies. In addition to synthetic materials such as Antron, it is also a good wing-post material for highly visible flies such as the Parachute Adams.

For many of my smaller minnow and darter patterns, calf tail is a good choice. Like quality deer tail, it offers the crinkly bulk without weight, but calf-tail fibers are not as dense as deer tail and make excellent short streamers. Calf-tail and guard-hair fibers from fur-bearing animals such as fox, squirrel, and raccoon are less than half the diameter of deer-tail fibers. They are also shorter and are my choice for flies tied on small hooks, such as small Deep Minnows for bonefish, Purple Darters, and Foxee Redd Minnows.

But calf tail can be frustrating to work with. You may have problems if you use many fibers in a clump and try to secure the bundle to the hook without first

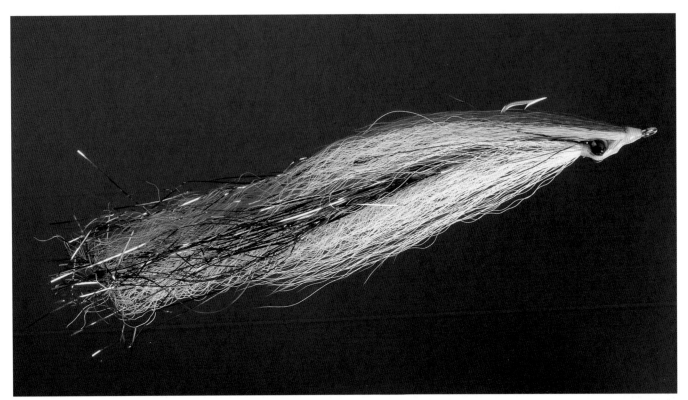

Synthetic hairs such as Kinky Fibre are excellent for big flies for which you do not have feathers that are long enough. This Half and Half was tied with Kinky Fibre.

removing the hair fibers of uneven lengths from the bundle. I prepare the bundle of hair by gripping it by the tips with one hand, and pulling most of the short fibers out with the other so that the remaining fibers are mostly the same length. Generally, the usable part of the bundle is about half of what was originally cut off. When calf-tail fibers are used sparsely on a fly, they move and act like deer-tail fibers. With calf tail, less is best.

SYNTHETIC HAIRS

Although natural fibers such as deer tail, calf tail, and fox-tail guard hairs are my favorite materials to use on streamer flies, synthetic hairs are sometimes a better choice. Synthetic hairs come in a wide range of diameters, lengths, and colors and are consistent in quality and durability. Some are translucent; others are more opaque. I like the translucency of Unique Hair or Super Hair for clear water and use these materials most often as substitutes for deer-tail fibers on my Deep Minnows. Unique Hair is a slightly softer, more supple version of Super Hair that is better suited for small flies.

When I don't have natural fibers for long flies—especially for Half and Halfs—I prefer to use Slinky Fibre or Big Fly Fiber. These two materials used sparsely still show bulk, silhouette, and length. At times, I integrate these materials with deer-tail fibers.

For smaller hooks or shorter flies, Craft Fur and Polar Fibre are good choices. The fibers of these materials are thin and tend to mat or tangle, but they can be brought back to shape with a fine stiff brush or fine-tooth comb. These materials should be used sparsely and not in bulky bundles. Treat this type of hair as you would calf-tail fibers, removing most of the short fibers from the cut-off portion of the bundle.

SYNTHETIC FLASHES

In the last four decades, manufacturers have introduced many new synthetic materials for fly tiers. Many of these materials have come and gone. Some were limited for use in a few patterns, but others, such as the synthetic flash materials, are perfect for a wide range of fly patterns.

Flash comes in many widths, shapes, and lengths, and in a variety of reflective qualities. I have experimented with many of the new flashes, but the ones I use repeatedly for my own flies are Flashabou and Krystal Flash. Flashabou flows and swims in the water without matting and reflects light as it undulates. Saltwater Flashabou is a wider ($^{1}/_{16}$-inch-wide), stiffer version of the regular Flashabou, designed for larger flies. Krystal Flash is an individual strand of Flashabou twisted into a permanently spiraled strand. The twist creates optical color illusions

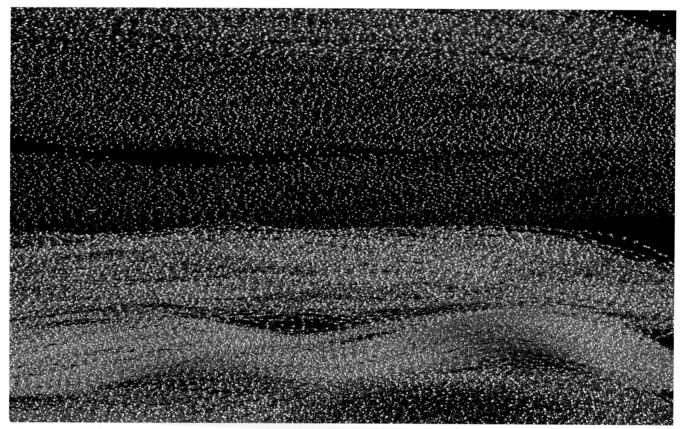

Above: Krystal Flash is twisted strands of Flashabou. It is available in many colors. Changing the flash color adds different highlights to your flies. Below: Flashabou is nontwisted strands of a supple flash material that is available in many colors. To give your flies extra motion, trim the Flashabou a little longer than the longest materials in your fly.

and a slightly stiffer fiber. Fish can see reflections from Krystal Flash from any direction.

If tied sparsely with Krystal Flash or Flashabou in the center of the hair, a fly takes on the transparent illusion of a live baitfish. Not only does the synthetic material add a little flash and flutter, attractive to fish, but it also simulates the lateral line that runs along many baits.

In my experience, flies with flash are more effective in most cases than ones without. But the amount of flash I use often depends on water clarity, fish species, and the other materials in the fly. When I tie flies with translucent materials, a little flash goes a long way. I have, however, tied and fished flies with as many as fifty strands of flash dangling out the rear and caught fish. With some species and in some water conditions, you can't use too much flash. In fact, I can say that I never used too much flash. As a fly tier, you can vary the amount of flash to suit your taste. You can also carry along a pair of scissors and trim out the flash material if you think you've used too much.

Water conditions play an important role in selecting colors and the amount of flash in the fly. I like gold for many types of conditions, especially if the water is off-color. I have fished for many species in many countries and have found that flies with gold flash material generally catch more fish than all other colors. Pearlescent is another good choice because it takes on the colors of the materials it is tied with.

To store my Krystal Flash and Flashabou, I hang it on a homemade caddy on my bench so that the colors I use frequently are readily accessible. Hanging them helps keep the individual strands from tangling. You can make your own caddy or purchase one. To make a nice loop from which to hang the materials, I double back the zip tie the material often comes on and whip-finish with heavy thread. I hang each bundle on the caddy with a paper clip inserted through the plastic loop. If you can't hang your flash materials because of space limitations or when traveling, cut off one side of the plastic bag that the material comes in. Having two open ends allows you to slide the materials in and out easily without damaging or bending the individual strands.

Make sure to cut strands of Flashabou or Krystal Flash in full lengths from the top of the bundle. You can

I store my flashes on a stand so they are always within reach.

ruin a package of the material by selecting and cutting various lengths from it. Then, when you need long strands, there will be none. If you do not use the full length after cutting it off the bundle, just use what you need and store the cut lengths for future use.

CHAPTER 2

Tying Techniques: Using Your Thread as a Tool

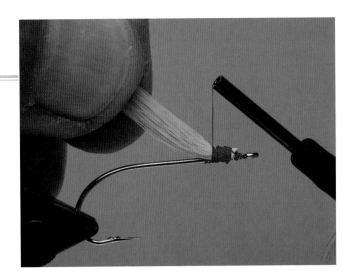

Many fine general fly-tying books provide basic instruction. Though the aim of this book is to focus on individual patterns, I hope that tying them will give you a solid foundation of tying techniques if you are a beginner and insight into my methods if you are more advanced. By tying these patterns, I hope you will become comfortable with and knowledgeable about working with deer tail, synthetic hairs, dumbbell eyes, epoxy, and general tying techniques. You will be able to apply these techniques to many different patterns, from small trout flies to large striper patterns.

Veteran tiers use their thread to make the materials they tie on their hooks behave the way they want. These techniques can help you become more expert and make your time at the vise more enjoyable and rewarding. Let's go over some thread-handling techniques that can help you tie materials to the hook shank more efficiently and manipulate materials to create better flies.

FOUNDATIONS

After you attach your thread to the hook, but before you tie any materials to the hook shank, it often helps to create a thread foundation. The foundation keeps materials from sliding and twisting around the slippery shank (unless you want them to, as when spinning deer hair) when you bind down materials or add weight to the shank. If you don't want to wrap the entire shank with thread, four to eight wraps around the shank near the tie-in point should do the job. For instance, after tying the dumbbell eyes on the Clouser Minnows, I always spiral-wrap loose turns of thread toward the hook eye and back to provide a base on which to tie the relatively slippery deer-tail fibers.

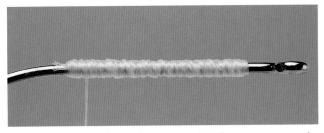

Loose open spirals around the hook shank provide a base on which to tie slippery fibers. Use these wraps to prepare the front end of the Clouser Minnow after you tie in the metallic eyes. Wrap forward to a point and then wrap the thread back over the preceding turns.

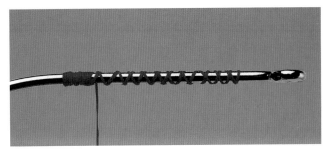

A good thread foundation keeps materials from twisting on the hook shank, and glue adheres better to a thread base than to a metal shank.

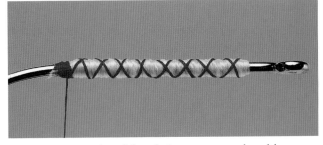

Use a screw-type thread foundation—an even thread base topped with an open spiral wrap—to help the glued material grip securely.

Thread foundations also help when you glue materials, such as popper bodies, to the shank. Glue adheres better to a thread base than a metal shank. In this case, use a screw-type thread foundation—an even thread base topped with an open spiral wrap—to help the glued material grip securely.

You can form several thread foundations to manipulate materials before or after you tie them in. Thread bumps are a good example. Their most common use is for splitting tails on dry flies, but I also use a bump to position the eyes on Clouser Minnows. Stack thread wraps carefully so they don't slide off one another as you build the bump. The best way is to build a thread pyramid.

Keep your bobbin as close as possible to your tying point by keeping a short thread length outside the bobbin. This technique saves time and provides better thread control when you gather and bind materials.

Thread bumps are necessary to properly position and tie in metallic eyes for the Clouser Minnow. Once you attach your tying thread, build a thread pyramid, decreasing the number of wraps in one spot as the bump gets larger.

MOUNTING MATERIALS IN PLACE
Pinch Wrap with Deer Tail

The snap, or pinch, wrap helps you place materials on top of the hook shank and keep them there as you secure them. With your thumb and forefinger, hold the material in position on top of the hook shank. Bring the thread up between your thumb and forefinger and pinch it between them. While pinching the thread, make a loose gathering wrap around the material with the thread and position the bobbin above the material or over the top of the hook. With steady tension, pull the thread down and out between your forefinger and thumb, trapping the material at the desired location. Keep holding the material in the same position during the pull to prevent the thread's torque from moving the material off the top of the shank.

Once you form the loop of thread in the pinch wrap, the key to positioning any material at a precise location on the hook is to pull the thread tight in an opposite direction from the tie-down point of the material. For example, if you want to tie in tail fibers on the side of the hook farthest from you, hold the materials against the far side, make a loose loop of thread, and tighten the thread by pulling it *toward* you. If you want to lash hackle fibers on the underside of the hook, such as for a beard on a classic wet fly, hold the fibers on the bottom of the hook, make a loose loop of thread, and pull the thread straight *up*.

1. Hold the material in position on top of the hook shank with your thumb and forefinger. Bring the thread up between your thumb and forefinger and pinch it. Make a complete turn with the thread around and under the material and the hook shank. Now position the bobbin and the thread above the hook shank between your thumb and forefinger.

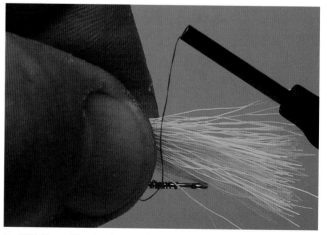

2. While still pinching the thread and material, begin lifting up on the thread, taking the slack out of the loop and drawing the loop tight against the bundle.

3. You can place material at any position on the hook shank. Just tighten the thread by pulling on the bobbin in a direction opposite from the material to tighten the material against the shank. Keep your fingers in the same position during the pull to prevent the thread's torque from pulling the material off the top of the shank.

PINCH WRAP WITH SADDLE HACKLES

Here is the sequence again with saddle hackles on the Half and Half. Note how the material is tied on top of the hook in step 4.

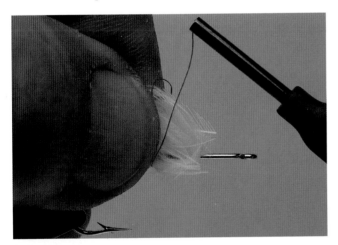

1.

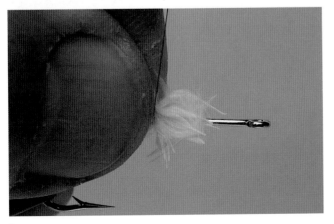

2.

3.

4.

THREAD TORQUE

The key to tying materials onto a hook is anchoring them where you want them, whether on top of or on the side of the shank. If you don't control thread torque as you wrap, your material will spin out of control. But if you can control thread torque, you can use it to your advantage when positioning materials. When tying on barbell eyes, I hold the eyes on the side of the hook nearest me and use the thread tension to pull the eyes on top of the hook. Thread torque is also helpful when spinning deer hair on the hook.

Thread torque is the tendency for thread to pull the materials around the hook in the direction in which you wrap the thread. You can either use it to your advantage or fight it. When tying in a bundle of hair such as deer-hair fibers, tie them in on the near side of the hook, and use the thread torque to pull them onto the hook shank.

Gathering Wrap

The gathering wrap is another essential technique when tying the Deep Minnow. When tying in deer-tail fibers, the gathering wrap collects the fiber butts and gives you greater control of their placement.

Place the material on top of the shank at the desired tie-in point. Bring the thread up and over the material, and gather it with moderate tension (slack wraps). Repeat with one or two more slack wraps. Then tighten the material to the hook shank by wrapping toward the hook eye. Never wrap back over the first gathering wrap; always wrap away from it.

1. Place the material on top of the shank at the desired tie-in point. Bring the thread up and over the material.

2. As you make a complete turn around the material, begin to gather it with moderate tension on the thread.

3. With the first few wraps, only apply a light amount of tension.

4. After several slack wraps, tighten the material to the hook shank by adding tension to the thread as you pull away from the position you want the material to be tightened down. After any material is positioned or set, never wrap back over the thread gathering wraps that were used to position the material.

5. The bundle tied in on top of the hook shank with a gathering wrap.

After you have tied the material on top of the hook shank and you want to wrap backward over the material and along the shank (when securing deer tail behind the eyes of a Clouser Minnow, for example), lift the material as you wrap to keep it on top of the shank.

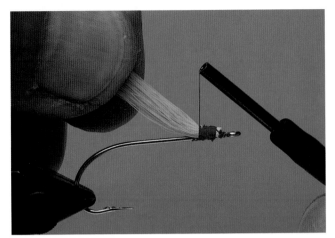

Lift up on your materials as your wrap back over them to keep them on top of the hook.

Fold-In Method

I use the fold-in method when tying in Flashabou and Krystal Flash on most of my patterns. The technique is fast, allows you to get better use of the material, and makes tying in strands at any position on the hook shank easy. The flash material streamlines with the other body materials, providing a more lifelike flash from a darting baitfish.

Fold five to ten strands of Krystal Flash or other flash material over the tying thread, and slide them down to the hook shank. Lift the material as you tie it down to keep it on top of the hook shank and previously tied-in materials.

1. Grasp the Krystal Flash bundle of full-length strands between your right thumb and forefinger. Leave a length of at least one full hook shank length of material protruding from your fingers.

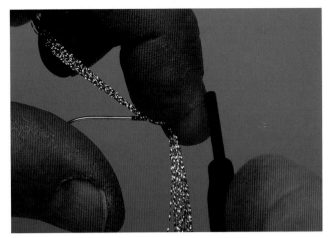

2. Bring the bobbin up above the hook shank with your right hand. As you rest the Krystal Flash on the taut thread, balance it with your right forefinger and let go with your thumb.

3. Still pressing the Krystal Flash tight against the thread with your left forefinger, grab the short strands with the thumb, place them between the thumb and forefinger, and pull them around the thread.

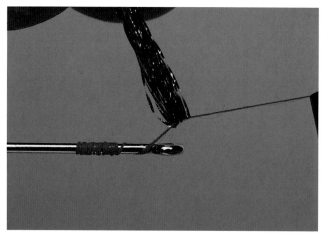

4. Pull your bobbin in the opposite direction from the Krystal Flash. Maintain tension on the bundle over the thread so you can control it.

5. Bring the bobbin over the hook eye, trapping the Krystal Flash on the hook shank. The Krystal Flash should be tied on the hook shank with the long fibers on the bottom and the short fibers on top.

6. Lift the material as you tie the folded portion on top of the hook shank.

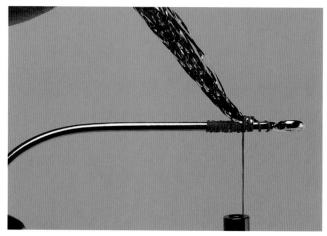

7. Continue lifting on the bundle as you lash it down.

8. Properly tied-in Krystal Flash using the fold-in method.

Cross-Wrap Mounts

Attach eyes to the hook shank with cross wraps. First place a bump of tying thread on the hook shank where you want the eyes to go. Place the barbell eyes perpendicular on the hook shank, tight against the rear of the thread bump, and make up to five cross wraps, first from right to left over the hook shank and the stem of the eyes. Repeat this process from left to right with the same amount of wraps. Apply even and hard tension with the thread as you wrap. Repeat this procedure three more times on each side, keeping steady tension when you change sides.

Cross wraps are not continuous figure-eight wraps, as you would use when tying in spinner wings. You cannot wrap metallic eyes securely to the hook shank using figure-eight wraps.

Make five or six circular wraps at the base of the cross wraps just under the eyes and above the hook shank. This constricts the thread and prevents the eyes from rotating. For added durability, you can add a drop of Zap-A-Gap on the thread wraps on the underside of the hook.

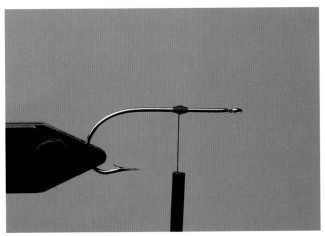

1. Attach your tying thread at a point one-third the length of the hook shank in front of the hook eye. Wrap a thread bump on the hook shank.

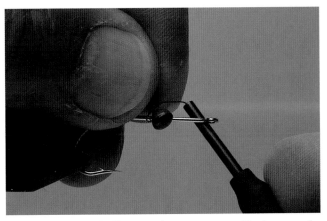

2. Place the barbell eyes almost perpendicular on the hook shank, tight against the rear of the thread bump, and make a turn of thread over the stem of the eyes to the other side of the hook shank, all while holding the eyes in place.

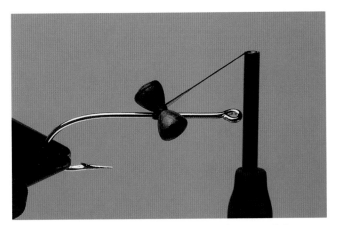

3. After two or more wraps, you can let go of the eyes. Continue making wraps from the side of the hook nearest you, over the stem, to the far side of the hook.

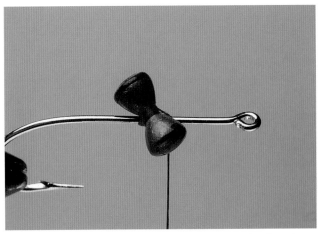

4. Make five to eight cross wraps on one side, then leave the thread on the far side of the hook.

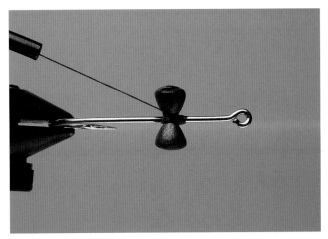

5. Straighten and center the eyes on top of the hook shank with your fingers. Bring the thread around the bottom of the shank and over the wraps in the other direction, from the right side of the eyes to the left. Wrap as many times as you did for the first set of cross wraps, applying even and hard tension with the thread as you wrap. Repeat this procedure three more times on each side, keeping steady tension when you change sides.

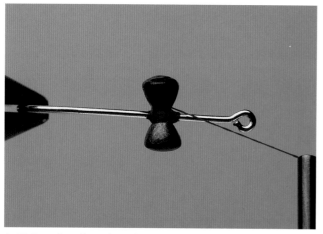

6. Bring the thread under the metallic eyes but over the hook shank, and circle the base of the cross wraps.

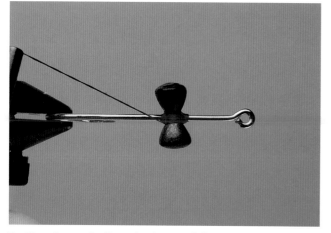

7. Continue circling the base of the cross wraps about five times. This constricts the wraps and tightens the eyes to the hook shank.

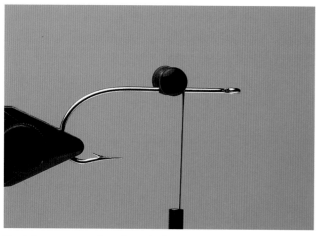

8. After you make the circle wraps, move your tying thread to a point in front of the eyes.

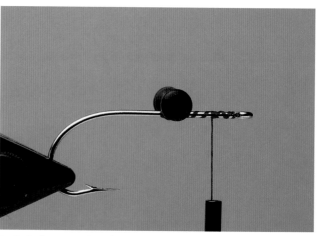

9. Spiral-wrap the thread to the hook eye and back to a point midway between the hook eye and the metallic eyes.

PART II

Baitfish:
The Clouser Deep Minnow and Variations

In both freshwater and saltwater fly fishing, baitfish are the most important food items to imitate if you want to catch fish consistently. In salt water and fresh water, from false albacore to smallmouth bass to trout, properly fished baitfish imitations are the best way to consistently bring the largest fish to the net—and sometimes the only way.

Just as trout anglers match mayflies with suggestive fly patterns, a match-the-hatch approach to baitfish imitations is an exciting and successful way to fish. Baitfish range widely in size, shape, color, and general habits, and understanding these characteristics well enough to tie and fish baitfish patterns effectively is a challenging part of fly fishing.

Most of the flies that I design to use on the Susquehanna River also work well in salt water, and in many areas of the country, Deep Minnows and Half and Halfs are as popular with saltwater anglers as they are with freshwater anglers. I think one reason is because smallmouth, like many saltwater species, take a range of bait sizes. On the Susquehanna River in Pennsylvania, where I fish and guide, blitzing bass and bait showering up from the water can, at times, rival the excitement of stripers and bluefish blitzing bait.

Choosing and fishing baitfish imitations is similar to matching and fishing insect hatches. Although you can tie on a suggestive pattern and catch fish, if you want a shot at smarter and larger fish, you need to understand what foods are on the table. Matching a baitfish's important characteristics and behaviors will increase your success.

Part of the Clouser Deep Minnow's success is its simplicity. It has become popular not only because it catches just about every species that swims, but also because it is a dead simple pattern to tie that can be adapted easily to each fishing situation. Anglers around the world fish the fly with equal results for freshwater and saltwater species. In different colors and in different weights, this fly catches tailing redfish or bonefish on the flats; stripers in the surf or in deep rips; and trout. This pattern is so effective and adaptable because it has become a style of tying, and anglers around the globe have been able to modify it slightly to catch fish on their home waters.

SIZE AND SHAPE

Most baitfish in fresh and salt water can be divided into categories based on their shape. For instance, a slim-profile Clouser Minnow of the appropriate length and color imitates small, slender baits such as spearing in salt water or black-nosed dace in fresh water. For broad, chunky baitfish, such as peanut bunker (salt water) or fallfish and gizzard shad (fresh water), the broader Half

Lefty Kreh lifts a striper he caught on a Half and Half. My favorite color combinations for this pattern are chartreuse and white and chartreuse and yellow. As Lefty says, "If it ain't chartreuse, it ain't no use." BOB CLOUSER PHOTO

and Half is the better choice. Bottom-dwelling species, such as freshwater darters and sculpins, often have broad heads tapering to narrow tails, and for them, I've developed calf-tail patterns specifically with their shape in mind. Whatever the species, paying attention to the overall shape of the baitfish you are trying to imitate is the first step to successful fly design.

On the Clouser Deep Minnow, the hair for the belly of the fly is attached in front and in back of the eyes to hold the hair in the shape of a minnow's belly. The top or back hair of the fly is tied only in front of the eyes. This angles the front portion of the hair upward, leaving the thinner rear hair fibers bent down during the stripping retrieve of the fly and touching the rear portion of the fly's belly hair. This bending together of the rear portion of the fly gives a thin rear profile with a deep front portion, which is an accurate representation of a real minnow's body. The natural taper of the deer-tail fibers helps achieve this.

Selecting the right baitfish imitation size and shape can often be the most important step to catching more fish. Many times, if your fly is a different shape or size than the naturals the fish are accustomed to, your chances of fooling fish diminish. For instance, if the area you intend to fish has an abundance of 1 1/2-inch-long bait-fish, you should probably choose a pattern of similar size. At times, however, fish prefer baits smaller or larger than the naturals, so carry several sizes of a particular pattern when you go fishing. I carry three sizes of each pattern.

One way to determine baitfish size is to collect samples with a seine or baitfish trap. Also, consider the time of year you fish. During certain periods of the year, especially from early spring to late fall, baitfish can grow at varying rates. Generally, baitfish are smaller early in the year and larger later in the year.

If you want big fish, give them groceries. Many trout anglers use relatively small baitfish imitations and then only catch small trout. Streamers flies can be tied on hook sizes from small size 10 to size 1/0 for trout. Although not the norm, on many trout fishing outings I have caught large trout on baitfish imitations five inches long.

Though I fish and guide on Pennsylvania's Susquehanna River, the patterns I have designed work well all around the world, in both fresh and salt water. On the Susquehanna, smallmouth can blitz schools of bait just like stripers.
BARRY BECK PHOTO

WEIGHT AND MOVEMENT

Though size and profile are critical, a baitfish pattern's weight can often determine its success. Not only does adjusting the amount of weight in a fly allow you to fish it at various depths, but the positioning and form of the weight influence the movement of the fly. On a Clouser Minnow, the metallic eyes positioned on the forward half of the fly helps imitate the fleeing movements of a panic-stricken baitfish.

In deep, dirty water, bonefish take large flies, such as this one caught on a chartreuse and yellow Clouser Deep Minnow tied on a circle hook. TOM WHITTLE PHOTO

One of the problems with conventional streamer patterns is that they stop moving during the retrieve when the angler is not stripping them. What baitfish would stop when chased by a predator? Predatory fish, especially the older, larger specimens, know when their target doesn't act the way it should. I developed the Clouser Deep Minnow to mimic the movements of a fleeing baitfish.

The amount of weight you should use depends on the type of baitfish. If you want to imitate bottom-dwelling baitfish, such as sculpin, darters, stonecats, baby catfish, or suckers, you need ample weight to put your fly on the bottom. If you are imitating free-swimming bait-fish, such as shiners, dace, chubs, or shad, you need less weight so you can retrieve your fly as it moves throughout the water column. I carry flies with different amounts of weight so I can fish at different levels and imitate the behavior of different baitfish.

PRESENTATION

Because the Clouser Deep Minnow represents a style of tying, the most effective presentation method is the one that best imitates the movements of the food you are trying to copy. It helps to understand the bait you are attempting to imitate and, if using a strip retrieve, to experiment with the retrieve to find out what works best. You can also fish the fly dead-drift with intermittent strips in flowing waters of rivers or in saltwater currents. The weighted part of the fly noses it down to the bottom. As it comes down through the currents and bounces along the bottom, it looks like an injured minnow trying to hide.

Just about every form of food that most species of fish eat, whether dwelling on the bottom or swimming through the water, has an escaping movement. No matter how quick a creature can go, it has to stop to hide or change directions. When it stops, that's the key for the fish to eat it. Most fish don't chase anything down and hit it running like a lion chases a gazelle. Fish, especially those without teeth, grab the bait when it stops. Fish with teeth—brown trout and barracuda, for instance—will strike a bait to injure it first. Most fish, though, like striped bass or smallmouth, take the bait when it's at a disadvantage. For example, a sculpin can dart from rock to rock, but it has to stop sometime. If the bait stops within eyesight of the predator, it's a goner. Susquehanna shiners hang in schools and when something comes after them, they try to dart and escape someplace. They have an erratic movement, but they have to stop to change direction or to go under the rocks and that's the chance for the predator to grab that fish. Clouser Minnows portray the movement of an escaping baitfish.

Many baitfish swim and move in different ways. Whether swimming around to feed or escaping a charging predator, each species has its own method of movement. Free-swimming minnows move in short, darting spurts or long, fast dashes. Bottom-dwelling baitfish dart erratically while seeking out places to hide. Both types, when escaping from a predator, head for cover on the bottom or somewhere in between.

Keep in mind what Lefty Kreh once said, "I have never seen a fleeing baitfish stop, face the predator, and ask to be eaten." Make your fly appear like it is trying to get away from an attacker. Move it *away* from a fish or fishy-looking lie.

SUSQUEHANNA STRIP

I developed a particular stripping method I call the Susquehanna Strip. This technique accelerates and pauses the fly during the retrieve so that when stripped back, it darts like a fleeing baitfish. With this technique, strikes increase tenfold over a steady stripping retrieve. Cast, and when the fly hits the water, drop the rod tip down to 6 inches from the water and make a long strip of 3 to 4 feet. As you start the strip, bring your arm back along your side. When your hand reaches your leg, quickly turn your thumb rearward to accelerate the strip. Ending

Clouser Deep Minnows and Half and Halfs are good flies to use for baby tarpon. Tom Whittle, a bamboo-rod maker from Harrisburg, Pennsylvania, holds a tarpon he caught on a Clouser Deep Minnow tied on a circle hook.
BOB CLOUSER PHOTO

the strip with a speed-up-and-stop portrays the erratic escaping movements of a scared baitfish. The quick acceleration frees the fly from the leader. The fly stops and turns down because of the weight of the metallic eyes. The strike comes on that drop.

This stripping method pulls the fly quickly toward you. The fly darts during the strip and dips during the pause, resembling the movements of an escaping baitfish. Lefty Kreh once told me that the reason my fly is so deadly is that it never stops moving, and neither does a baitfish that is trying to escape a predator.

A smallmouth will not follow behind a fly. It stays on the bottom and follows the fly below it. When the strip is complete and the fly starts to drop, the smallmouth swims in front of it and comes at it almost headfirst to intercept it. A smallmouth doesn't inhale its prey from the rear. The dropping motion of the fly during the pause of the strip triggers the fish to strike. I have never caught a smallmouth on the strip, only during the pause between strips. Detecting a strike like this can be challenging at first. Many other predators, such as tarpon, jack, striped bass, and largemouth bass, also intercept the fly as it drops during the pause of the strip. I think the pause and drop trigger many fish to take the fly.

When I strip the line with my left hand, I move my right hand (holding the rod) across my body so it's in line with my left. This prevents line from chafing my right forefinger, which I use to control the line. Holding on the right side and stripping to the left cuts grooves in your fingers.

DRAG AND MENDING

A dry-fly fisherman's worst enemy is drag. When drag takes over, it pulls your fly and you lose control of it. Drag also happens underwater. Baitfish, whether bottom dwelling or free swimming in the middle of the water column, move in a particular manner that you can't copy with drag on the line. With drag, the fly just swings and pulls and moves unnaturally through the water.

Drag is caused by water pressure on the fly line, causing the line to move downstream faster than the fly. When the fly rod, line, and fly are not moving downstream at the same speed, drag occurs. To control drag, keep your cast as close to you as possible, and try not to cast over water with both fast and slow current speeds. If necessary, try moving to a different location for a better presentation. You can also control drag by mending. After you cast, lift the rod upward while lifting the curve of the fly line off the water, and cast the line back upstream far enough to pause the drag in the drift of the fly line. When you are making the upstream mend, try not to disturb or interrupt the drift of the fly. Many times you will have to make as many as three or five mends just to control one drift over a three-foot span of bottom.

WADE- AND BOAT-FISHING TECHNIQUES

Fishing a Clouser Minnow with a strip retrieve effectively while wade fishing is difficult and not as efficient as fishing it from a boat drifting at the current speed, but it can be done. To strip the fly back and make it look like bait coming across the current, darting and twisting and acting hurt, you need to mend your line upstream in between the strips. As soon as you cast your fly across current, throw an upstream mend in your line, strip the fly a few times, and repeat another mend. The upstream mend relieves the fly from the unnatural pull of the line and leader by the downstream current. With the fly free from the leader, it is loose and bounces and jigs in the current. After a few strips, throw another upstream mend. If I don't get another hit after a few strips and a few mends, I do not fish my fly through the rest of the drift. I pick it up and cast it back into what I think is the sweet spot or the fish's lie. I situate myself about ten feet below the lie and cast upstream, which gives me more room to work that area productively than if I stood straight across from it.

Another approach I use is to fish directly upstream to my target. I cast into the lie and strip the fly back downstream. I like to get 30 or 40 feet below the target, cast, drop the rod tip, and strip the fly as fast as the current is moving. This is a very effective method, but it is also a lot of work.

If you cast across current and do not mend, the fly swings around at a relatively steady speed but does not stop and drop, because the line and leader are always under tension.

In a boat, I like to drift with the current, so there is no drag to contend with and mends are not often necessary. All you have to do is manipulate the fly. When drifting in a boat, I tell my clients to cast in a straight line from them to the shoreline or a little downstream for the best retrieves. When you anchor and cast across current, you need to mend your line as you would when wade-fishing.

COLOR

Color, though not as crucial as size, profile, and weight, can be important. Baitfish colors vary with habitat, light reflection, water depth, and water clarity. Most colors turn dark below certain (relatively shallow) depths and as clarity diminishes. I don't know why certain colors sometimes work better than others. I just know that they do, so I always carry several colors of each fly.

Many baitfish species emit basic reflective colors. These colors usually appear as various pearlescent shades, gold, silver, and even chartreuse. Not only do the basic colors change, but their hues also vary and include shades of gray, brown, olive, white, green, purple, and blue.

CHAPTER 3

The Original Clouser Deep Minnow

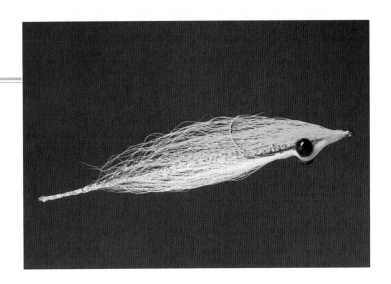

Back in the late 1970s, my friends and I pinched split shot on deer-tail streamers to emulate the motion of a jig because, hands down, fishing with a jig is one of the most effective ways to catch fish. We tied the first prototypes of the Deep Minnow on streamer hooks with different-size Water Gremlin split shot crimped at the head of the hook. We'd either pinch the split shot on the shank behind the eye and then tie the fly around it or modify a finished fly by pinching the shot on the nose. These early flies dived and dipped like jigs and caught more fish than the flies without the split shot, but they looked so ugly that I didn't want to show them to people. They were pretty rough looking.

In 1985, Tom Schmuecker of Wapsi Fly Company in Mountain Home, Arkansas, sent me an assortment of lead barbell-shaped eyes made from molds he had developed. I took some of them out of the package, laid them on my fly-tying table, and wheels started turning in my mind. These new eyes could add weight and look great on a deer-tail streamer.

In the middle of the smallmouth season in late August 1985, I added these eyes to popular bass patterns such as Woolly Buggers, Zonkers, and marabou leeches and had immediate success. In 1986, I tied more of these flies in different color combinations. The Susquehanna has a bass season of only three months, which doesn't leave much time for experimenting with various fly patterns.

In 1987, I added these eyes to my favorite deer-tail streamers, the ones I previously had tied with split shot. With the lead eyes lashed to the hook and painted to look like baitfish eyes, the old pattern took on a new look. The most important component of the new fly was now in place. The eyes provided the weight that made the fly dip and dart in the currents like a natural baitfish escaping a predator. I also slimmed down my original bucktail pattern, because friends who first tested the pattern told me that the sparsely dressed ones were more effective than the heavily dressed ones. Those new flies caught more smallmouth on one trip than any other fly I ever used.

I tied these flies in a few color variations to imitate the local baitfish. Gray and white imitated the silver shiner, and brown and white imitated the golden shiner or sculpin. I tied them all on size 4 hooks and they were 1 3/4 inches long, the length of most of the bucktail jigs that worked best on the Susquehanna River.

In early July 1988, I had extremely positive reports from the few people who were fishing the new flies. I had shared the fly patterns with my son, Bob Jr., and my buddy John Lowell, and they both told me they were

For bonefish, I carry pink and white, tan and white, and chartreuse and white Clouser Minnows in sizes 2 to 6 with a range of weighted eyes, including light plastic bead chain for skinny water.

Bob Clouser Jr. holds a false albacore that took a Clouser Deep Minnow. BOB CLOUSER PHOTO

catching smallmouth when nothing else was working. I phoned Lefty Kreh. Excited, I told him about this new fly with the barbell eyes that the smallmouth wanted to eat. He came up to fish in August of that year, and when he entered my shop, I dropped a dozen in his hand. He looked at the flies and asked with astonishment, "Are they done?"

Lefty and his friend went out on the river around 10:00 that morning. I was to join them around 3:00. When we met up, I asked Lefty whether he was catching anything on the flies I gave him.

"Nope," he said.

I looked on the end of his leader. "Well, you don't even have one of my flies on."

"I'm testing other flies to see if I can find one that will do as well as yours!"

I asked his buddy, who had an ear-to-ear smile, how he was doing with the new fly. He said, "You know, this is the first time I have outfished Lefty Kreh!"

Lefty has since told me that he has caught more than eighty-six species on the Clouser Deep Minnow.

Lefty first wrote about the Clouser Deep Minnow in *Fly Fisherman* in 1989, which helped spread the word about the pattern. Here's how he tells the story:

The Susquehanna River near Middletown is perhaps a half-mile wide, with a gentle flow and a bottom paved in limestone rock—perfect habitat for smallmouths. We anchored in a deep pool near a ledge that rose almost to the surface. I tied on Bob's fly, made a long cast, and allowed it to almost dead-drift. It had traveled less than ten feet when a smallmouth grabbed it. I'm not sure how many fish I caught that day, but Bob's new fly fired my imagination as no fly has for years. . . . This is the best underwater pattern I have fished in decades. In fact, I don't know of a better underwater fly. . . . Clouser's Deep Minnow looks and swims like a minnow, but best of all it's a streamer you can cast easily, and it sinks like an anvil in a swamp.

COLOR COMBINATIONS

The first two Clouser Deep Minnows I tied both had white bellies. One had a brown back with gold Krystal Flash in the center, and the other had a gray back and silver Krystal Flash. Since the pattern was new, I was

When tying Clouser Deep Minnows with three colors, such as in the flies at the top and bottom, use sparse amounts of deer-tail fibers. Shown are brown, green, and white (for baby smallmouth); chartreuse and yellow; and purple, gray, and white Clouser Deep Minnows.

Sam Talarico releases a catfish that took a Clouser Deep Minnow. Susquehanna River catfish also feed on the surface when the whitefly hatches. BOB CLOUSER PHOTO

searching for a name for it. I phoned Lefty and asked him what he thought I should call it. Without hesitation, Lefty said, "Well, it was tied by Clouser and looks like a minnow and it goes deep. Call it a Clouser Deep Minnow." Lefty and I dubbed these the golden shiner and the silver shiner. After that, Lefty, my son Bob Jr., and I started developing various color combinations because on certain days one pattern would work well, and on another it would not. On different days with different light conditions, the fish preferred different color combinations.

Over a period of about two years after the initial development of the fly in 1987, I developed certain fly patterns for certain times of the year. During low and clear water, when the brighter colors do not work as well, I like to use flies with more subdued colors. My baby smallmouth pattern, with a white belly, green middle, brown back, and subdued flashes such as bronze and gold Flashabou, has saved the day during late September

and October when the water is low and clear. Also at this time, brown and tan, olive and yellow, and brown and tan mixed together are good combinations.

For most of the anglers involved in testing the fly, chartreuse and white and chartreuse and yellow became favorite color combinations, and they have become, for the most part, the most effective all-around patterns. If you could have only a few colors, these combinations would be your best bet. You could catch fish with these colors 90 percent of the season.

For two straight years, I experimented with an all-white Clouser Minnow whenever I fished salt water, and I caught fish every place I went. That convinced me that I was carrying too many color combinations on my saltwater trips.

Of all the people who fish the Clouser Deep Minnow, I probably carry the fewest color combinations: chartreuse and white, chartreuse and yellow, tan and white, pink and white, and all white. The chartreuse and yellow, with gold Krystal Flash, is one of my favorites, especially for striped bass, smallmouth, and a host of other species. When other colors aren't working, that's the color I usually go to, and it generally works. I don't know what's so magical about that color combination, but it works well in all water conditions.

Over the years, this fly has increased in popularity as anglers have learned about its effectiveness on gamefish. It can be tied on hook sizes 7/0 through 6 for saltwater and warmwater species. The most popular sizes range from 1/0 through 6. Clouser Deep Minnows and their variations cover the general range of baits, including menhaden; small sand eels and rain baits, which attract stripers, bluefish, and albacore; and small shrimp or baitfish imitations for many flats species, such as redfish and bonefish.

For bonefish, my three favorite colors are tan and white with gold flash, pink and white with pearl flash, and chartreuse and white with pearl flash. I carry these in three sizes—2, 4, and 6—and tie some with heavy eyes and some with plastic and metal bead-chain eyes. Which I use depends on water conditions and whether the fish are spooky.

Hook sizes 1 through 6 are the general range for most warmwater species, such as smallmouth and largemouth bass. Clouser Minnows tied on smaller hook sizes, from 6 to 10, work well on the trout streams and lakes across country. I like to tie my favorite trout Clouser Minnows in subdued colors on 4XL hooks in sizes 4 through 10. For smallmouth, I use hook sizes 2 through 6, although at times larger smallmouth like size 1 and 1/0.

Clouser Deep Minnow

Hook:	Size 2 Mustad 3365A, 3366, S71S SS, or Tiemco 811S
Thread:	6/0 light cahill Uni-Thread
Eyes:	$^6/_{32}$-inch-diameter ($^1/_{30}$-ounce) lead Wapsi Presentation Eyes, painted red with black pupils
Belly:	White deer-tail fibers
Flash:	Silver Krystal Flash
Back:	Chartreuse deer-tail fibers

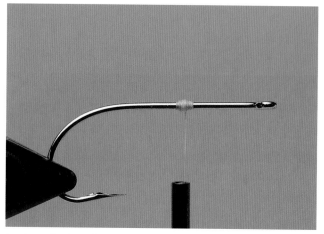

1. Attach the thread at a position one-third the hook shank length in front of the hook eye. Build a bump of thread for the metallic eyes. Attaching the eyes at this point on the hook leaves plenty of room to tie in the deer-tail fibers and keeps you from crowding the eye.

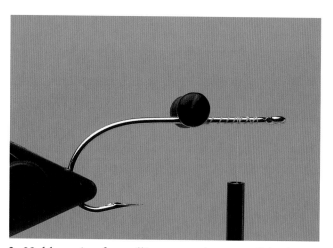

2. Hold a pair of metallic eyes at the rear of the bump, and attach them with a series of cross wraps. Secure the eyes by making a circle wrap under the eyes and over the hook shank. Spiral-wrap the thread to a point behind the hook eye and then back to a position halfway between the metallic eyes and the hook eye.

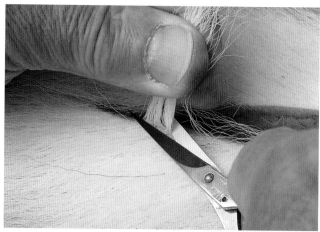

3. Lift a bundle upward from the skin at a 90-degree angle, and cut the fibers as close as you can to the skin. Lifting the fibers perpendicular to skin before cutting them helps you get an even bundle. Cut the fibers from the top two-thirds of the deer tail. (See the section on deer-tail hair in chapter 1.)

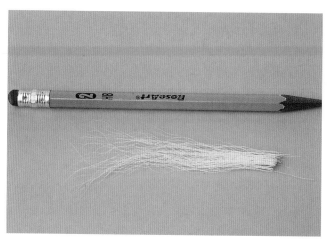

4. The bundle should be about half the thickness of a wooden pencil. It's important to use only a small bunch of fibers. A sparse amount of deer-tail fibers provides the necessary profile. On patterns with three or more colors of deer-tail fibers, bundles should be even sparser.

5. Remove the shorter fibers from the butt end of the bundle by holding the tips of the fibers and pulling loose fibers out from the butt. Transfer the bundle to your other hand, hold the butts, and remove any long or stray fibers from the tip. It is not necessary to use a hair stacker for preparing the deer-tail bundle. You want the bundle to have the natural taper.

8. As you come around the material and hook, tighten the bundle by lifting up on the thread. The gathering wrap collects and positions all the butts of deer-tail hair on top of the hook shank. Make sure there are no deer-tail fibers protruding over the hook eye.

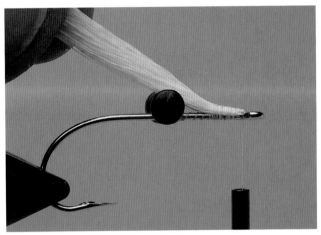

6. Measure the bundle of deer-tail fibers so that they are two to two and a half times the length of the hook. Transfer the fibers to your other hand, and trim the butts so that they are even.

9. As you slowly tighten the gathering wraps, lift the rear of the deer-hair bundle. When I do this, I pull hard enough to lift up the eye of the hook. Wrap the thread toward the hook eye, making sure you do not wrap back over the initial gathering wraps. Do not wrap back to the metallic eyes; you want a space between them and the beginning of the tie-down wraps of thread on the deer tail. The fibers should be tied in a nice, neat bundle so they lie between the dumbbell eyes and not flared past the width of the dumbbell eyes.

7. Hold the bundle of deer-tail fibers at a 45-degree angle, so the butts touch the hook shank in front of the thread. Begin a loose thread wrap to gather the bundle on top of the hook shank.

10. With the thread positioned behind the hook eye, bring the bobbin back toward the bend of the hook, under and to the rear of the metallic eyes on the near side of the hook. In one continuous motion, tie over the deer-tail fibers to secure them to the hook shank behind the eyes.

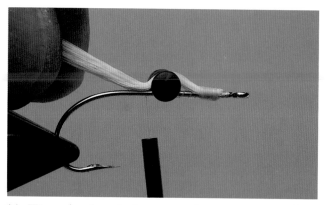

11. Wrap the thread, three complete wraps, around the deer-tail hair and the hook shank while lifting up the bundle of deer-tail fibers. At the same time, apply light pressure to the wraps of the thread.

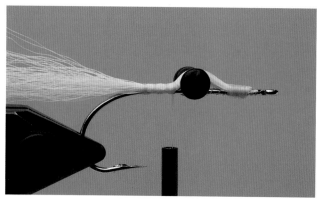

12. Spiral-wrap the thread toward the rear of the hook to a position above the hook point, making three complete turns of the thread. Spiral-wrap the tying thread forward to the rear of the metallic eyes.

13. Move the thread forward under the metallic eyes to a position behind the eye of the hook, and wrap one or two complete turns around the hook behind the eye. It's important to use only as many thread wraps as you need to secure a material or anchor the thread.

14. The completed belly of the fly.

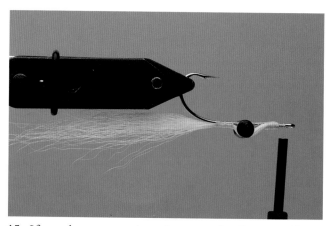

15. If you have a rotating vise, turn the fly over. If not, take the fly out, flip it over, and insert it back into the vise. When doing this, be careful the thread doesn't move from its original position behind the hook eye.

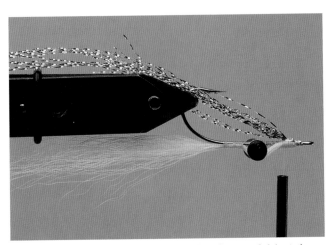

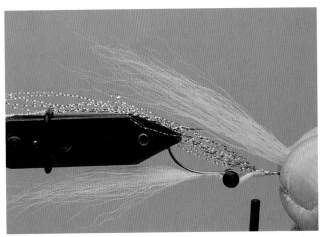

16. With the thread behind the hook eye, fold eight to twelve strands of Krystal Flash around the thread and tie it down on top of the secured deer-tail hair. Lift up the bundle of Krystal Flash as you tie it down. Fold it over the thread, with one side about a third shorter than the other. There should be enough flash on the long side to extend slightly past the tapered ends of the deer tail on the rear of the fly. The short ends of Krystal Flash should be long enough to go past the hook point when tied back.

18. Cut a bundle of chartreuse deer-tail hair slightly thicker than the bundle selected for the belly portion of the fly. Remove loose fibers from the butts, trim the butts, and measure for length. The length should equal that of the deer-tail fibers used for the belly. Trim the butts again if you need to adjust the length of the fibers. These fibers form the back of the basic two-tone Clouser Deep Minnow. If you were tying a fly with two colors on the underside of the hook, you'd need to cut the size of this bundle in half.

17. Cut the Krystal Flash so that it is $1/2$ to 1 inch beyond the tips of the deer-tail fibers. When the flash protrudes beyond the fibers, the fly reflects more light and has more action in the water. Part both the long and short fibers so that they are equally distributed on both sides of the hook point.

19. Position the butts of the deer-hair bundle directly on top of the Krystal Flash. Place the butts forward of the thread, and make two loose turns with the thread around the butts of the deer-tail hair. Slowly increase the pressure on the thread to secure the deer-tail fibers.

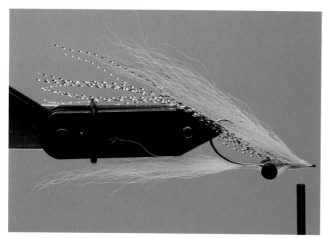

20. Wrap the thread forward to a point just behind the hook eye, adding pressure to the thread as you wrap. Apply sufficient tension to the thread wraps so that the hair does not pull out of the completed fly. Form a neat head with the thread, using minimal thread wraps to avoid a bulky head.

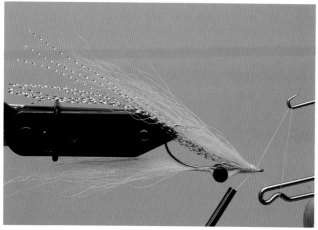

21. Whip-finish the thread and remove the fly from the vise.

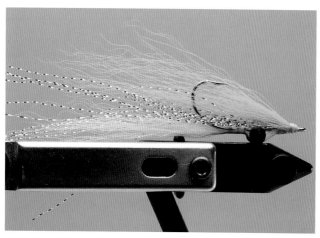

22. The Clouser Deep Minnow ready for epoxy.

23. For a more durable head and fly, cover the exposed thread and the area in and around the metallic eyes with a five- or thirty-minute epoxy.

24. Squeeze out equal parts of two-part epoxy, and mix them evenly.

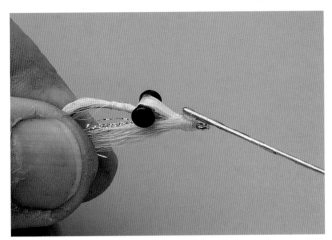

25. Apply epoxy to the top of the fly and the spiral wraps along the white deer tail. I prefer a blunt applicator, because sharp bodkins can catch on the deer-hair fibers. Don't worry if a little head cement gets on the fibers near the thread wraps; that's a good thing and seals the head for extra durability.

27. If you use five-minute epoxy, set your fly in a rotating drier wheel to dry or turn it by hand. You need to use a rotating drier if using epoxy with a 30-minute or more curing time.

26. Also apply epoxy to the gaps between the deer-tail fibers and the metallic eyes. The epoxy not only protects the eyes, but also secures them to the hook shank and makes a sleek head for the fly.

CHAPTER 4

Fur Strip Clouser

The Fur Strip Clouser is an easy adaptation of the deer-hair pattern that takes advantage of the proven fish-catching properties of rabbit strips. Rabbit strips move enticingly in the water, and the individual fibers breathe in the current, making them excellent for patterns in fresh or salt water.

The Fur Strip Clouser tied longer and chunkier than the deer-hair minnow is a good choice to imitate eels, hellgrammites, and large baitfish, such as peanut bunker in salt water or alewives in fresh water. I tie this pattern on a wide range of hooks to catch everything from largemouth bass and big pike to snook. It is deadly for trout when tied on hook sizes 4 through 8.

In very clear water conditions, I fish a Fur Strip Clouser with light eyes, such as $^4/_{32}$- or $^5/_{32}$-ounce metallic eyes on hook sizes 2 through 1/0. Bass take the fly when it is dropping. Northeastern anglers report that a Clouser tied with a yellow rabbit strip is a good pattern for weakfish and bass. To spruce up your fly, you can purchase barred rabbit strips or use a black or brown permanent marker to add bars.

Wide fur strips work best on large Clouser Minnows. These are often sold as Magnum strips. For smaller flies, you can use regular Zonker strips made from rabbit,

Left: Fur Strip Clousers imitate everything from large baitfish to eels, making them excellent flies for pike, muskies, and stripers. Here, Dan Blanton releases a California Delta striper. Above: Small Fur Strip Clousers in different color combinations work well for Great Lakes steelhead, either swung through a pool or dead drifted to fish you can see holding. All-white flies with silver flash are especially effective.
BOB CLOUSER PHOTOS

mink, or pine squirrel. In addition to offering lots of other fly-tying materials, craft stores and fly shops often sell whole tanned rabbit skins in different colors. If you buy them whole, you can cut them yourself by first stretching the skin tight, using a clipboard, nailing it to a board, or securing it in a sewing loop, and then cutting the skin side with a razor blade. You must be careful not to lay the fur side on a table top or any object while cutting the strips. You only want to cut through the hide, not the hair. You can make several cuts at once by taping a set of box knives together. For thick strips, leave every other blade out. Cutting them yourself is an economical way to go if you have the time.

Fur Strip Clouser

Hook:	Size 2 Mustad 3365A, 3366, S71S SS, or Tiemco 811S
Thread:	6/0 gray Uni-Thread
Eyes:	$^6/_{32}$-inch-diameter ($^1/_{30}$-ounce) lead Wapsi Presentation Eyes, painted red with black pupils
Belly:	White deer-tail fibers
Flash:	Pearl Flashabou
Back:	Gray deer-tail fibers
Tail:	Grizzly-colored rabbit fur strip, $^1/_4$ inch wide

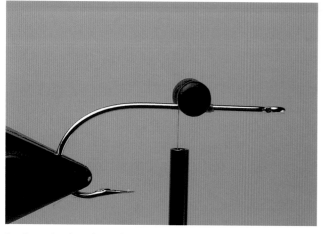

1. Attach the thread at a position one-third the hook shank length in front of the hook eye, and form a bump with the thread. Attach the metallic eyes. For this fly, we are using a size 2 hook and $^6/_{32}$-inch-diameter metallic eyes.

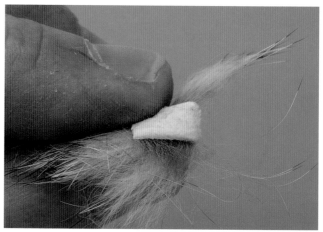

2. Select a $^1/_4$-inch-wide, 8-inch-long rabbit-fur strip, and fold back the skin portion $^1/_2$ inch.

3. Cut a small slit through both ends of the strip with scissors where it is folded back.

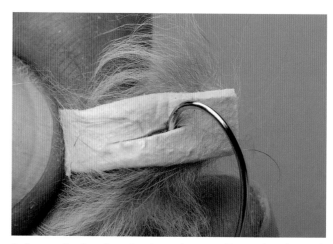

4. Insert the hook point into the cut slit on the skin side of the fur strip.

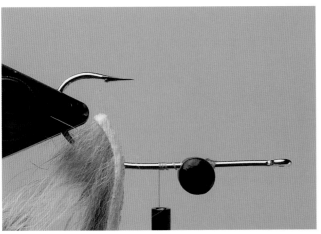

5. Insert the hook into the vise upside down. Make sure the skin side of the fur strip faces the metallic eyes.

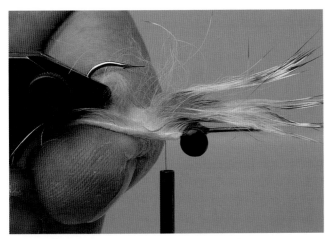

6. Position the end of the fur strip so it butts up against the metallic eyes. Moisten the fur fibers with saliva or water, and stroke them forward over the eyes with your fingers. This clears the area for your thread wraps.

7. Take several thread wraps around the skin, trying not to tie down too many fibers. Stroke them forward as much as you have to. You can also use a bodkin to pull out any hair fibers trapped by the thread.

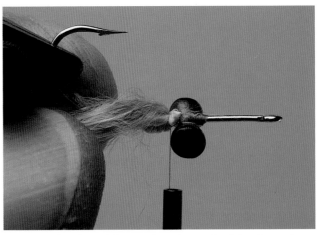

8. Bring the thread forward to the end of the fur strip, so that it is positioned behind the metallic eyes. Wrap back toward the hook bend with your thread, securing the rabbit skin and fibers so that they point back toward the hook bend.

9. After you secure the fur strip behind the eyes, rotate the hook in your vise. Spiral-wrap the thread forward to a point just behind the hook eye, and then back to a position halfway between the hook eye and the metallic eyes.

10. Select a bundle of white deer-tail fibers, and clean out the short fibers from the butt section of the bundle. The length of the deer-hair bundle should be about two to two and a half times the hook length. Trim the butts evenly when cutting the bundle to the proper length.

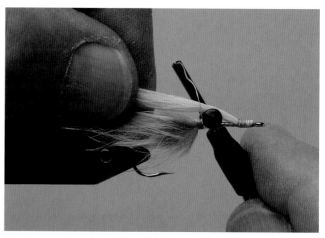

13. Bring the thread back behind the metallic eyes, and in one continuous motion, wrap over the deer-tail fibers to lash them to the hook shank. As you bring the thread back with one hand, lift the deer-tail fibers with the other.

11. Position the deer-hair butts so that they are against the hook eye at a 45-degree angle.

14. Tie down the bundle of deer-tail hair behind the metallic eyes.

12. Using a gathering wrap, tie the butts down on top of the hook shank. Make sure no fibers block the hook eye when you position the thread behind it.

15. For this pattern, you need to flare the deer-tail fibers to create a broader profile. Push on the bundle (over the thread wraps) with the flat side of your scissors or your thumb to spread the fibers.

16. Bring the thread forward, under the metallic eyes, to a point behind the hook eye, and anchor the thread with one complete wrap around the hook.

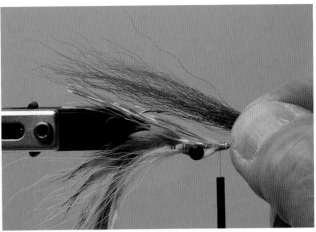

18. Select a bundle of gray deer-tail hair about half as thick as a pencil. It should be as long as the white deer-tail fibers.

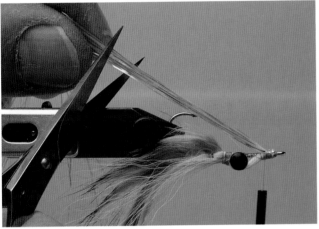

17. Turn the hook over in the vise, making sure that the thread has not moved from the position in the previous step. Select eight to twelve strands of pearl Flashabou, and tie them down on the hook shank using the fold-in method. Cut the Flashabou about two times the hook length. Position the thread midway between the rear of the hook eye and the metallic eyes.

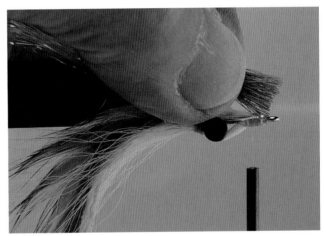

19. Position the bottom edge of the trimmed deer-tail butts at a 45-degree angle in front of the hook eye.

20. Tie down the gray bundle of deer-tail fibers using a gathering wrap. Starting at the first wrap, bring the thread forward toward the hook eye. Wrap back over the thread if necessary to form a neat head.

21. Whip-finish the fly. Cut the rabbit strip to length by sawing the skin side with one scissors blade. The rabbit strip should be longer than the deer-tail fibers.

22. The finished fly, ready for head cement or epoxy. Apply cement or epoxy on the exposed thread of the head, behind the metallic eyes, and in and around the eyes.

CHAPTER 5

Rattle Clouser

When I first saw rattles, I thought they were going to be the ticket for muddy water. Bass are triggered by noise, so I figured rattles in my flies would help me catch more fish when the river was dirty. I experimented a lot with rattles in flies when they first came out in both fresh and salt water, and I didn't see any increase in any strikes except in clear, deep water. This was completely opposite of what I had expected. When smallmouth fishing in ten feet or more of clear water, in crystal-clear lakes as well as clear rivers, after two or three strips of the fly, I would see a bass come up—somewhere, not right near the fly—and dart as if it were looking for something. If the fish happened to see the fly, it would often move to take it.

Spinnerbaits and rattles in spinning lures provide a continuous noise that both alerts the fish and allows them to track the direction of what they perceive as bait. With spin-fishing gear, you can continuously retrieve a lure so that it never stops moving and constantly makes noise. When you fish a fly with a rattle, however, the only times it makes noise is when you begin and end the strip. You can pull that fly two or three feet before it makes another noise. If you try to fish it slow and with short strips, you can make an almost continuous noise,

Above: Rattles come in many forms. Snip the ends off the rattles that come with a tip on them, such as these black ones. Left: Many anglers like to use rattle flies for redfish (shown here) and snook in salt water. I also use the Rattle Clouser for smallmouth in deep, clear water.
BOB CLOUSER PHOTO

47

but then the fly doesn't act right. But it's clear to me from my observations that the rattles only alert the fish to the fly. It's the visual, and not the audible, trigger that makes the fish hit the fly. For those times when a rattle in a fly catches more fish—deep, clear water—I always make sure I have a few Rattle Clousers with me.

The first time I tied one of these Rattle Clousers on a tippet of my client's leader, we were over some deep water, ten feet or more, and the bottom was not visible. My client cast out the rattle fly, and as he stripped it back toward the boat, I watched in amazement as a small-mouth swam into view, searching for the source of the noise. Some smallmouth came from 4 to 8 feet away to chase that fly. I think the rattle fly had an advantage over one without a rattle.

I had fished over these deep-water areas before and had to use heavily weighted flies to get strikes. Lighter flies without rattles would run only about a foot or two under the surface and did not get any attention from the smallmouth. I think the smallmouth heard the rattle when the strip was stopped prior to a sharp acceleration of the fly at the stop. When a smallmouth heard the noise, it would come up looking for whatever made it, spot the fly, and go for it.

I've fished for redfish quite a bit, but I don't have as much experience with them as some anglers who claim that rattle flies account for increased hookups. I have never taken a rattle fly off when it was catching fish just to test another fly. I can speculate, though, that a Rattle Clouser might be a good thing to try for any species that will take a fly on short strips, which allow the fish to track the rattling noise, or a fly that is fished dead drift so that it rattles as it bounces along the bottom.

Rattle Clouser	
Hook:	Size 1/0 Mustad S74S SS
Thread:	6/0 fire orange Uni-Thread
Rattle sleeve:	³/₈-inch-diameter Corsair
Rattle:	Any rattle designed for lures
Body:	Wide metallic silver Estaz
Wing:	Pink over white deer-tail fibers
Flash:	Pearl Flashabou

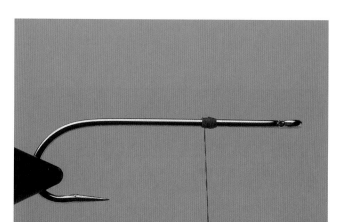

1. Attach the thread at a position one-third the hook shank length in front of the hook eye. Tie a bump of thread for the metallic eyes.

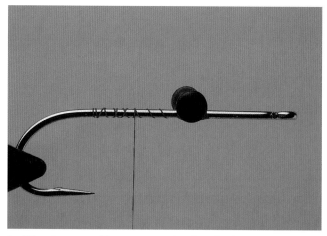

2. Tie the metallic eyes to the hook shank with cross wraps. Spiral-wrap the thread back to the hook point and then back to a point halfway between the metallic eyes and the hook point. These wraps form a base for the Corsair material.

3. Prepare a 4-inch section of ³/₈-inch–diameter white Corsair tubing by holding it between the thumb and forefinger of your left hand, and squeezing it lightly as you pull it through the thumb and forefinger of your right hand. Place the end of the tubing behind the metallic eyes.

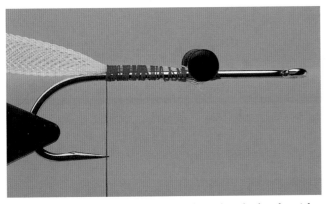

4. Tie the tubing down on top of the hook shank with a gathering wrap or pinch wrap. Wrap your thread toward the metallic eye and then back toward the hook point to bind down the Corsair.

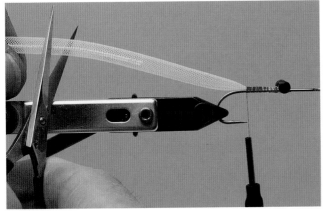

5. If you did not precut the Corsair, trim it to length now. You waste less material by not precutting it, but trimming it takes more time if you're tying these flies in batches.

6. Plastic rattles come in various shapes and sizes. If yours has a peg attached to one end, remove it with wire cutters.

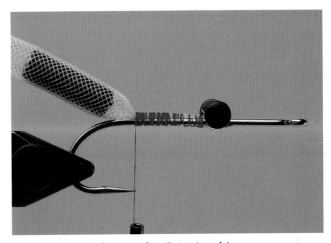

7. Insert the rattle into the Corsair tubing.

8. Tie in an 8-inch-long piece of extra-wide metallic silver Estaz above the hook point.

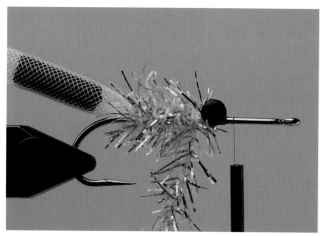

9. Spiral-wrap the Estaz forward to a point behind the metallic eyes.

10. Make one turn with the Estaz under and over the stem of the metallic eye nearest you.

11. Wrap the Estaz from the front of the metallic eye that is on the opposite side of the hook one full turn around the stem of the eye.

12. Top view of the previous step.

13. Wrap the Estaz one full turn around the hook shank in front of the metallic eyes, and then tie it down.

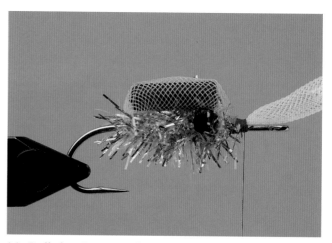

14. Pull the Corsair tubing and rattle forward, over the metallic eyes, and tie them down on the hook shank in front of the metallic eyes. Lift up on the tubing with one hand when you lash it down.

toward the hook eye, and then back to a point just in front of the spot where you made your first gathering wrap over the deer hair.

15. Turn the hook upside down in the vise.

18. Move the thread to behind the hook eye. Tie in eight to twelve strand of pearl Flashabou, using the fold-in method, and trim it so that the long strands extend about $^1/_2$ inch beyond the deer-tail fibers.

16. Select a bundle of deer-tail hair about half as thick as a pencil, and measure it for length. The bundle should be two to two and a half times the hook length. Pull loose fibers from the base of the bundle, and trim the butts.

19. Wrap the thread back over the flash to a position between the hook eye and the metallic eyes.

17. Starting at the halfway point between the metallic eyes and the eye of the hook, tie down the butts of the deer tail with gathering wraps, applying increasing thread pressure as you wrap the butts down. Wrap your thread

20. Select a bundle of pink deer-tail hair containing about one-quarter more fibers than the white. Measure it for length; it should be the same length as the white. Pull the loose fibers from the bottom of the bundle, and trim the butts evenly.

22. Form a neat head and whip-finish.

21. Tie down the bundle of pink deer-tail fibers on top of the secured Flashabou using a gathering wrap.

23. Complete the fly by coating the head with epoxy or a durable head cement.

CHAPTER 6

Super Hair
Deep Minnow

I use synthetic hairs on my Deep Minnows for a variety of reasons: durability, consistency, length, and translucency. According to some scientists and my own observations, in cold, clear water, fish's eyes are sharper, allowing them to distinguish things better than in warm water. Translucent flies tied with synthetics seem to catch more fish in cold, clear water conditions, and perhaps this is because they look more realistic than other flies to fish, which are able to see better at this time. I think this is also why anglers have to use lighter, 4- to 6-pound-test tippets in the clear water of fall but can use 8- to 12-pound-test tippets in spring and summer.

In cold, crystal-clear water, translucent flies attract more strikes than the deer-tail Deep Minnows. On the Susquehanna River, the last two weeks of September and October are the best times to fish Deep Minnows tied with Unique Hair or Super Hair. The most productive fly for Susquehanna smallmouth is a tan and white or gray and white Super Hair Deep Minnow with a few strands of gold flash. Often, as the day progresses, certain color combinations stop working. If you are not catching fish, change either the size or color of your pattern.

Tom Earnhardt, an angler experienced with fish species worldwide, often fishes a synthetic-hair Clouser Minnow for false albacore. He has written that he likes synthetic flies with silver and black painted eyes on hook sizes 4, 2, and 1/0 in green and clear (with silver flash) and chartreuse and clear (with gold flash) Ultra Hair.

Synthetics are the perfect choice when fishing for bluefish, because flies tied with synthetic hair will last for a few more fish than those tied with bucktail.

When I tie Clouser Deep Minnows with Super Hair and Unique Hair, I use a method called high tying, which separates each bundle or color from the others. Although they all seem to be tied together as one, each

Use synthetic hair as a substitute for deer-tail fibers in low, clear water or for saltwater fish such as bluefish and snook (shown here). LEFTY KREH PHOTO

bundle remains separate from the other. Other synthetic materials also make good Clouser Minnows, including Kinky Fibre and Kraft Fur.

KINKY AND SLINKY FIBRE MINNOWS

I use Slinky Fibre for flies that are too long to be tied out of deer tail. Slinky Fibre and similar synthetics, such as Kinky Fibre, create a bulky profile with a sparse amount of material. The wide kinks in the strands of material create the illusion of width or bulk. Kinky Fibre is easy to work with, fishes well, and seems to create less tangles than some of the other synthetics. It does not absorb water, making it easier to lift out of the water to make a cast. This same property also makes it float, however, and you must add weight to the fly so it will sink quickly.

When working with Slinky Fibre, tie the Deep Minnow using the same steps as with deer-tail fibers. After you whip-finish the fly, take it from the vise and trim with scissors to a baitfish shape as done for the Super Hair Deep Minnow, cutting the fibers in staggered lengths. This not only creates the shape, but also helps prevent fouling. Pull the flash material away from the fly so you do not cut it accidentally.

Blue-over-white or gray-over-white Super Hair Clousers are perfect imitations for the small silversides that false albacore like this one often feed on. Linda Heller, Harker's Island, North Carolina. BOB CLOUSER PHOTO

With a few modifications in tying techniques, you can easily substitute synthetic hair for deer-tail fibers in Clouser Deep Minnows. The top two flies are tied with Super Hair, and the other fly is tied with Kinky Fibre.

With this method, you can tie a range of flies, from small trout patterns to large saltwater flies. This material rarely fouls. The only downside to this material and other synthetics is that once it is kinked or bent, it will stay in that shape. I recommend carrying or storing these flies in individual plastic sleeves, available in two sizes: 1½ by 9 inches and 1½ by 5 inches. These sleeves do a great job of protecting all baitfish patterns, whether they are tied with synthetic or natural fibers.

KRAFT FUR MINNOWS

Kraft Fur and similar products are available in various colors and can be opaque or translucent, depending on the manufacturer. They also come in a variety of textures, some coarse and some smooth to the touch. They range from less than 1 inch to around 3 inches long.

This type of hair is manufactured with a cloth backing. You can find fibers suitable for tying on one side of the cloth. The fibers vary in length and can be used by cutting off a bundle with a pair of scissors. For a bundle of longer fibers, there is a special way to cut the fibers from the backing. I find that the following method is the best way to gather a bundle of tapered fibers.

1. With a pet comb or brush, comb all the fibers in the direction of the taper so that they lie down neatly against the backing.
2. Place the patch of fur on your left leg above the knee, with the tip ends of the fibers pointing to the left. The fibers are easier to control if the patch is lying on a contour instead of a flat surface.
3. Grasp a bundle of fur with your left hand, preferably from the left bottom corner of the patch. Lift it upward from the patch and cut it off with scissors, move your left hand to the right, grasp another bundle, and cut it off as close to the patch as you can. Repeat this step one more time. Make sure you remove bundles of fibers by moving across the patch, and not from bottom to top.
4. Grasp all three bundles together in your left hand, holding them near the tips. Pull out the short fibers from the butt ends with your right hand. Use these fibers as you would deer tail, following the tying instructions for the Deep Minnow tied with deer tail.

One disadvantage to this material is that it mats after a few fish. Some anglers who like the way this material looks and don't mind the inconvenience, suggest carrying a small brush to smooth out the fibers when they mat. You could also use another hook to comb the fibers.

Super Hair Deep Minnow	
Hook:	Size 2 Mustad 3365A, 3366, S71S SS, or Tiemco 811S
Thread:	Danville clear monofilament, fine
Eyes:	6/32-inch-diameter (1/30-ounce) lead Wapsi Presentation Eyes, painted red with black pupils
Belly:	White Super Hair
Middle:	Pink Super Hair
Flash:	Pearl Krystal Flash
Back:	Gray Super Hair

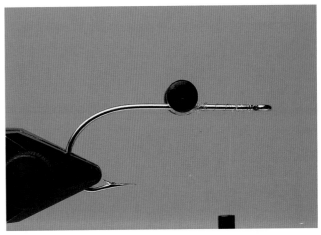

1. Tie in and secure the metallic eyes with monofilament nylon thread. Spiral-wrap the thread to a point just behind the hook eye. These screwlike wraps provide a surface for the material to grab onto so they don't slip on the bare hook shank. Many synthetic materials are slippery, so this step is essential.

2. Cut a sparse bundle of white Super Hair, and trim the butts even. At this point, you do not need to worry about length, so no measuring is necessary. Hold the butts at a 45-degree angle so they just touch the rear of the hook eye. Use a gathering wrap to bind down the synthetic fibers.

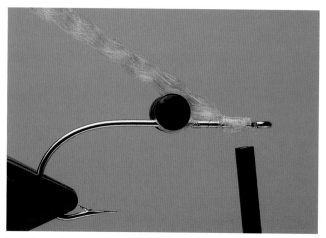

3. Wrap the monofilament thread to a point just behind the hook eye.

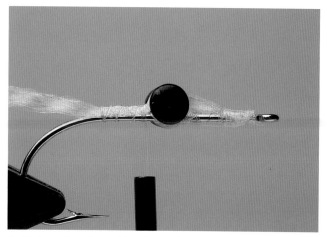

4. Bring the thread back under the metallic eyes, and wrap over the bundle of Super Hair. As you wrap back toward the area above the hook point with the thread, hold the Super Hair in your other hand, and bind down the fibers in one smooth step. Take several wraps around the hook shank to anchor the thread. Take three or four wraps toward the hook bend and back toward the metallic eyes to secure the Super Hair.

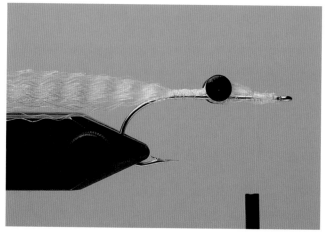

5. Position the thread halfway between the hook eye and the metallic eyes. Turn the hook over in the vise, making sure the thread doesn't move from its position.

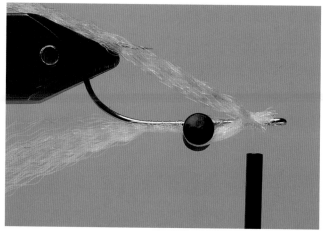

6. Cut a small bundle of pink Super Hair slightly thicker than the white (belly) bundle, trim the butts, and tie it to the hook.

7. Tie in the Krystal Flash using the fold-in method. Wrap back over the Krystal Flash and then forward, one turn forward of the tie-in point of the pink Super Hair.

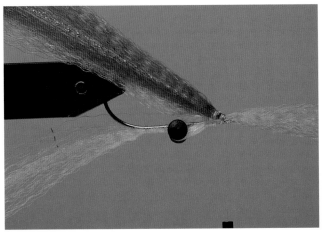

8. Tie in the gray Super Hair about 3 inches before the butts, so that the butts hang forward over the eye.

9. Fold the butts extending forward over the hook eye back, and tie them down. This creates extra bulk in the front of the fly. If you want a slim version, tie in the last bunch of Super Hair the same way as the others.

10. The finished fly needs to be trimmed.

11. At a little more than one hook shank length from the bend of the hook, cut the forward half of the fibers at a 45-degree angle.

12. Also trim the back half of the fly's top at a 45-degree angle.

13. Turn the fly, and cut the other half of the fibers at the same angle. This trimming step makes every fiber in the fly a different length and helps the fly maintain its shape. You don't want your flies to be droopy, because the materials tend to wrap around the hook shank. Cutting them in this manner prevents fouling.

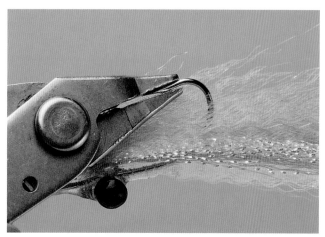

14. Debarb the hook. Try to debarb the hooks at the bench so you don't forget during the excitement of fishing.

15. Add cement or epoxy to the monofilament thread wraps of the fly. Also cover in between the eyes, and put a drop on each side of the fibers behind the thread. As you work the glue into the fibers, pull on them.

The finished fly should show nice separation of the synthetic fibers. High-tying materials creates bulk while also preserving the different colors of material.

CHAPTER 7

Half and Half

I needed a large fly in my box to imitate the fallfish (up to 18 inches long) on the Susquehanna River, which the smallmouth over three pounds eat. It may be hard to believe, but big smallmouth eat fallfish up to a foot long, and if you want to catch those big fish on a regular basis, you need to give them groceries.

The Clouser Minnow didn't have the bulk or the flashy sides that I felt were necessary for a good imitation, so I combined the rear saddle hackles and collar of Lefty's Deceiver for length and bulk at the rear of the hook and built the Clouser Deep Minnow onto the front portion of the hook. I also added lots of flash to the fly. The Half and Half was born.

The first time I fished this fly was on the Susquehanna River during a blitz of big smallmouth. It was right after daybreak, a few hours before my clients for the day arrived. As the sun rose and the water became silvery, I spotted feeding smallmouth herding gizzard shad up against a rock ledge. I slowly poled the boat into casting range, made the cast, and watched as the Half and Half entered the water and slowly descended toward the bottom. It sank about 2 feet, and as the fly disappeared from sight, I set the hook into a four-pound smallmouth. The school of bait moved, and again the bass pushed them to the surface. Still within range, I cast the fly to the target. As it sank, I had another big smallmouth on. I was a happy fly tier.

I have a hard time keeping a successful fly secret, so when I had the chance, I phoned Lefty Kreh and Bob Popovics and told them of the pattern's success. Bob was scheduled to fish with me the following month, and I primed him with promises of a big smallmouth on this new fly.

Bob was excited as we motored up to the Highspire Turnpike Bridge, where I knew some big bass lived in the deep holes near the pylons. I anchored the boat off to the side of one of the piers. "All you have to do is throw this big fly about 10 feet in front of this pier," I told Bob. "When it hits the water, don't do anything, just watch it fall."

Bob is an excellent caster, so the fly landed right on target. He paused on the retrieve and let it fall. As the fly fluttered down through the water column, a dark form darted out and inhaled the fly.

Lefty Kreh has since used the Half and Half in South America, Australia, and numerous other places and has caught more than two dozen species on it, including large grouper, big pike, 30-pound-plus stripers, peacock bass, largemouth bass, smallmouth bass, tarpon, snook, snapper, and barracuda, to name a few. He claims that it is his favorite pattern when he wants a fly with lots of

Bob Popovics holds a Susquehanna smallmouth that took a Half and Half. BOB CLOUSER PHOTO

The Half and Half pairs the qualities of the Lefty's Deceiver and the Clouser Deep Minnow. It is a winning combination for everything from smallmouth to stripers. Lefty Kreh (left) and Bob Clouser (right) with a striper they caught on a Half and Half. BOB POPOVICS PHOTO

flash, a bulky silhouette, and weight. He uses the fly with barbell eyes from size extrasmall to extralarge. His favorite color combination is the same as mine: chartreuse and white.

The Clouser Deep Minnow is the ideal imitation for most slim-bodied baitfish, such as spearing, sand eels, and many freshwater baits. The Half and Half provides the other part of the equation, with the flash and silhouette of many large-bodied baitfish, such as peanut bunker, menhaden, shad, and the many broad forms of panfish and other robust species in fresh water. The Clouser Deep Minnow and Half and Half in a range of sizes, colors, and weights will cover most of your bases for weighted flies in fresh and salt water.

Effective color combinations in fresh and salt water are all white, chartreuse and white, red and white, blue and white, and gray and white. In salt water, the Half and Half is a great imitation for bunker and other large baitfish. Albacore, even when feeding on smaller baits, love Half and Halfs. Capt. Jack Eudy, a North Carolina albacore and striper guide, likes to use the red and white Half and Half for albacore.

Half and Halfs are designed to imitate large, broad-profiled baitfish, and the long saddle hackles tied off the bend of the hook make realistic large flies. When you can't find natural materials long enough, use synthetic fibers such as Kinky Fibre (middle fly).

The Half and Half is a pattern style that can be tied with various materials and other methods. For instance, you can change the color of the collar, use grizzly hackles instead of white ones, or tie in the flash materials behind the hook eye, as in the Clouser Deep Minnow instructions.

Half and Half

Hook:	Size 2/0 Mustad 34007
Thread:	Gray Danville Flymaster Plus
Eyes:	$7/32$-inch-diameter ($1/24$-ounce) lead Wapsi Presentation Eyes, painted red with black pupils
Flash:	Silver Flashabou
Saddle hackles:	5- to 7-inch-long strung hackle
Collar:	White deer-tail fibers
Belly:	White deer-tail fibers
Back:	Gray deer-tail fibers

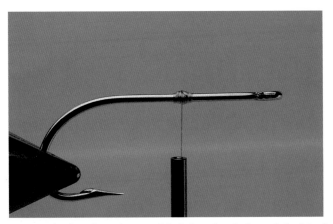

1. Attach the thread one-third the shank length behind the hook eye, and build a thread bump for the metallic eyes.

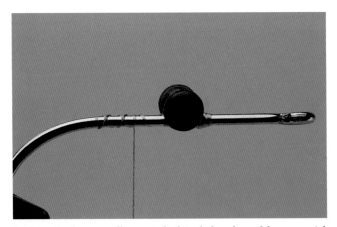

2. Attach the metallic eyes behind the thread bump with cross wraps. Spiral-wrap the thread back to just above the hook point, and spiral-wrap it forward to a position halfway between the hook point and the metallic eyes.

3. Select six white saddle hackles about three to four times the length of the hook. Prepare them by making two separate stacks of three. Place the two separate stacks together with the insides of the saddle hackles facing each other, creating a knife blade effect. Trim the stems at the butt ends of the saddle hackles, leaving all the parts of the feathers on the stems; do not clean off the fibers.

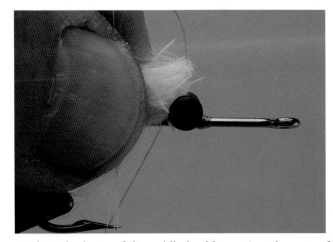

4. Place the butts of the saddle hackles against the rear of the metallic eyes. Pinching the hackle stems and the hook shank, bring the thread up between your thumb and forefinger to pinch it as well. Pinching all three things, begin taking a loose wrap over the butts of the saddle hackle.

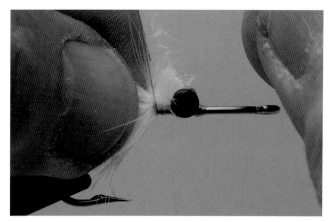

5. As you complete the loose wrap around the hook shank and the saddle hackle butts, snap up with the thread, tightening the hackle butts to the shank.

6. Wrap the thread forward to a point behind the metallic eyes.

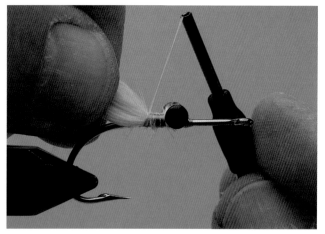

7. Wrap the thread back to where you attached the hackle butts with the pinch wrap, grasping all the saddle hackles between your thumb and forefinger, and lifting them up as you secure them to the hook shank. Lifting them up like this keeps them on top of the hook.

8. Holding up the saddle hackles, wrap back to a position above the hook point and then forward toward the rear of the metallic eyes, forming a neat, closely wrapped platform of tying thread. This provides a nice platform on which to tie the deer-tail fibers.

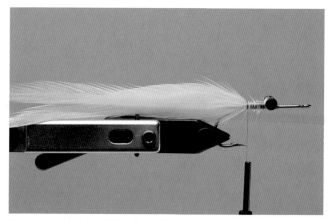

9. The saddle hackles should be secured to the top of the hook shank and look like a knife blade.

10. Cut a bundle of white deer-tail fibers half as thick as a pencil from the deer tail. Remove all the short deer-tail fibers from the butt end of the bundle. Measure the fibers so they are two times the length of the hook. Trim the butts evenly.

11. Hold the butts of the white deer-tail fibers behind the metallic eyes.

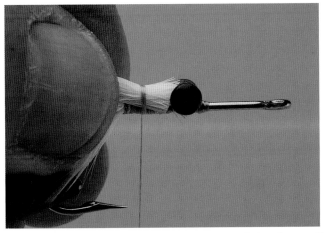

12. Take two loose turns of thread around the deer-tail bundle.

13. Without tightening the thread wraps too much, flare the bundle with your thumb or flat side of a scissors blade. This forces the deer-tail bundles to follow the path of the thread wraps, creating a collar of deer-tail fibers around the body of the fly.

14. After you form the collar, wrap the thread forward to the rear of the metallic eyes.

15. Bring the thread in front of the metallic eyes, and spiral-wrap it to a point behind the hook eye back to a position halfway between the hook eye and the metallic eyes.

16. Select a bundle of white deer-tail fibers about half the thickness of a pencil, and measure it so that it is three times the hook length. Remove any loose fibers from the base of the bundle, and trim the butts even.

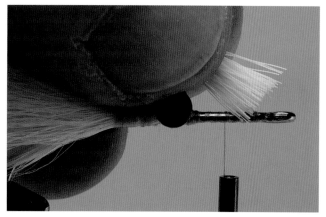

17. Hold the butts of the white deer-tail bundle at a 45-degree angle so they are just touching the rear of the hook eye.

20. Bring the thread under the metallic eyes while holding the deer-tail bundle with your other hand.

18. Tie the fibers on top of the hook by making two loose gathering wraps around the bundle, slowly adding pressure to the thread wraps as you lift up the thread. Wrap forward to a point just behind the hook eye.

21. Loosely wrap the thread around the deer-tail bundle.

19. This photo gives you an idea of how long the deer hair should be in relation to the saddle hackles. The deer-tail fibers should slant at a 45-degree angle back toward the bend of the hook, and the fibers should be neat and contained within the metallic eyes.

22. Spread the deer-tail bundle by pressing down on the two loose thread wraps with a flat scissors blade.

23. The bundle should flare. To help spread the fibers, you can push the bundle down with your thumb.

24. After you have spread the fibers, secure the deer-tail bundle with even thread wraps, forming a collar behind the metallic eyes. Bring your thread under the metallic eyes to a point directly behind the hook eye.

25. Turn the hook upside down in the vise, making sure the thread is still behind the hook eye.

26. Tie in fifteen to twenty strands of silver Flashabou behind the hook eye, using the fold-in method. Lift up the Flashabou with one hand, and secure it by wrapping back from the hook eye to a point between the metallic eyes and the eye of the hook.

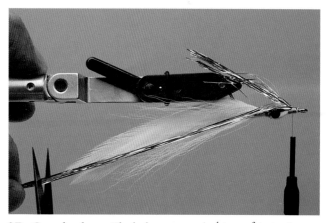

27. Cut the long Flashabou strands $1/2$ to $3/4$ inch past the tips of the saddle hackles.

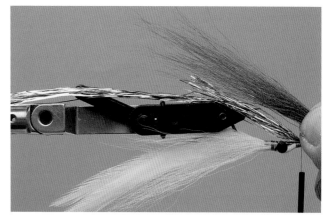

28. Select a bundle of gray deer-tail fibers about half as thick as a wooden pencil, and measure it so that it is the same length as white deer-tail belly. Remove loose hairs from the bottom of the bundle, and trim the butts evenly.

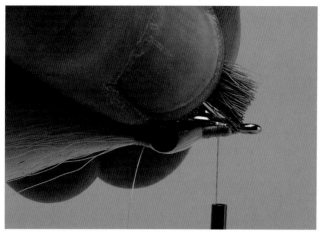

29. Hold the butts at a 45-degree angle to the hook shank, with the butts touching behind the hook eye.

30. Tie in the bundle with gathering wraps, and secure it by wrapping forward with increasing pressure. Form a neat head and whip-finish.

31. Coat the head, eyes, and thread wraps behind the eyes with epoxy, and place the fly in a rotating dryer to ensure that the head is coated evenly.

CHAPTER 8

Foxee Redd Minnow

The Foxee Redd Minnow is a version of the Clouser Deep Minnow that has become a staple for many species of fish. I do not leave home without this one, and I carry it in a variety of sizes. It has become my favorite fly for trout and carp. It's also effective for redfish, snook, and bonefish.

I was looking for some type of material to make a shorter Clouser that would give me the same type of

The Foxee Redd Minnow is my go-to fly for carp. Cast the fly within two or three feet of a feeding fish, and let it sink to the bottom. MIKE O'BRIEN PHOTO

action in the water as the longer deer tail did. If you shorten deer tail and tie it on the hook shank, it is stiff and has no action in the water. I had always liked the colors of red fox tail guard hairs and decided to give them a try.

My first attempt was a disaster. Fox tail has a lot of soft underfur, which makes good dubbing for nymphs and dry flies. I cut off a clump of the hair and tied it in without first removing the underfur. The fly had a bulky head, looked horrible, and matted when wet. One day it dawned on me to remove the underfur and use just the long guard hairs. To make the fly look like a sculpin, which is brown with black streaks and mottling, I used fur from different parts of the tail.

Most fox tails available in fly shops come from pen-raised foxes. Tails from pen-raised foxes do not have consistent colors but are useful. Ideally, you want fibers from a wild prime red fox tail, which has hairs with black tips and reddish brown middles. On a good fox tail—like on a good dry-fly chicken neck—the guard hairs are short at the base of the tail and get increasingly longer toward the tip. Look for a black circle of guard hairs at the base of the tail that swirls around the tail toward the tip.

When using fibers from fox tail, or any fur with short or soft underfur, you need to remove the short and soft fibers from the bundle, leaving only the longest hairs. Doing this helps make neat, small heads and also prevents fibers from pulling out on the completed fly.

To remove the soft underfur, hold on to the tips of the clump, and brush the base of the fibers with a wire dog brush until you are left with just the guard hairs. With all the underfur removed, red fox-tail guard hairs don't tangle or mat, and they make a small, neat Clouser Minnow that looks just like a deer tail pattern going through the water.

The Foxee Redd Minnow imitates sculpins and crayfish in freshwater rivers and also looks enough like a shrimp that it is a deadly pattern for redfish and bonefish, especially over dark marl bottoms. Lefty thinks it looks like a baby carp or rock bass. I love to fish this pattern for trout (sizes 2–8) in coldwater rivers and carp (sizes 2–6) on the Susquehanna from late July to September.

Carp fishing is all sight fishing along muddy shorelines and shallow gravel bars. When I get a client who can cast well and wants to try to catch a carp, we look for fish rooting in the mud in the shallows and don't cast the fly unless the fish's head is down, feeding, and its tail is up. We observe the fish to get a sense of the direction in which it is feeding and try to cast in front of it so that it sees the fly. To know when to set the hook, watch the carp. When its yellowish orange mouth opens, it shines as though somebody turned on a lightbulb. When that light goes out, tighten up your line.

Foxee Redd Minnow	
Hook:	Size 8 Mustad R74
Thread:	6/0 light cahill Uni-Thread
Eyes:	$4/32$-inch-diameter ($1/80$-ounce) lead Wapsi Presentation Eyes, painted red with black pupils
Belly:	Cream-colored guard-hair fibers from a red fox tail
Flash:	Gold Krystal Flash and bronze Flashabou
Back:	Black-tipped red fox guard hair fibers with a reddish brown area below the black tips

Bob Popovics lifts a heavy Susquehanna River carp that ate a Foxee Redd Minnow. BOB CLOUSER PHOTO

Wild red fox tail (shown here) has bands of guard hairs with black tips starting at the base of the tail and spiraling toward the tip. The guard hairs closest to the base are short and good for short flies. The guard hairs get increasingly longer toward the tip.

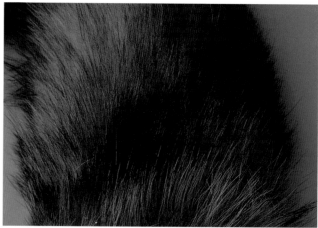

1. Fox tail has a variety of colors in it. On a natural wild red fox tail, an area of guard hairs near the rump encircles the tail in a spiral from the butt to the tip. These guard hair fibers have black tips, reddish brown centers, and grayish butts. At the base of the tail is a cluster of black-tipped guard hair fibers (shown here) suitable for 4XL hooks in sizes 8 and 10. The black-tipped guard hairs spiral around the tail to the tip. As on a high-quality dry-fly cape, the guard hairs get longer toward the tip. On the underside near the butt end of the tail, you should find lighter, buff-colored guard hairs. These lighter-colored guard hairs are also distributed throughout the tail in various lengths. Use these lighter fibers for the belly section of the Foxee Redd Minnow.

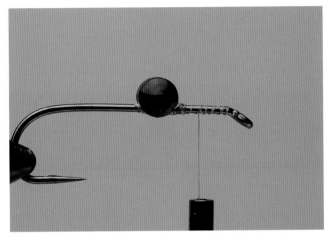

2. Attach the thread at a point one-third the hook shank length in front of the hook eye. Build a thread bump for the metallic eyes. Attach the metallic eyes to the hook shank with cross wraps, and make circle wraps around the base of the cross wraps. Spiral-wrap the thread to the hook eye and back to a point midway between the end of the hook eye and the metallic eyes.

3. Select a clump of light-colored guard hairs mixed with the soft underfur, and cut the clump from the skin.

4. Remove all the soft underfur by holding the tips of the guard hairs and scraping the butts of the clump with a dog-grooming brush.

5. To ensure that you have enough guard hairs, you need to select a relatively large clump, because red fox tail has a lot of underfur. This underfur makes nice reddish brown dubbing.

6. Measure the red fox guard hairs to one and a half times the length of the hook. Trim the butts evenly.

7. Hold the red fox fibers at a 45-degree angle so that the butts are just touching or slightly behind the hook eye. Make a full turn of thread around the butts with a loose gathering wrap, bring the thread directly above the clump of red fox guard hairs, and pull up.

8. Wrap down the butts toward the hook eye, stopping when you reach the beginning of the eye. Wrap back to the point shown in the photo.

9. Bring the thread back under the metallic eyes and over the clump of red fox fibers with one hand, while holding them with your other hand. Make two full turns over the red fox guard hairs as you lift up the bundle of guard hairs.

10. Spiral-wrap the thread back to a position above the hook point, and make two full turns of the thread around the red fox guard hairs and the hook shank. Spiral-wrap the thread forward to a point just behind the metallic eyes. Bring the thread in front of the metallic eyes, and take one full turn around the hook shank.

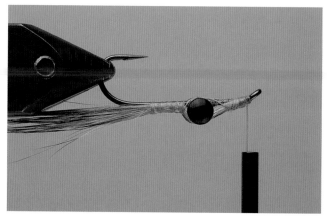

11. Turn the hook upside down in the vise. Wrap the thread forward to a point behind the hook eye.

12. Tie in six to eight strands of gold Krystal Flash behind the eye of the hook with the fold-in method. Position the thread in back of the hook eye.

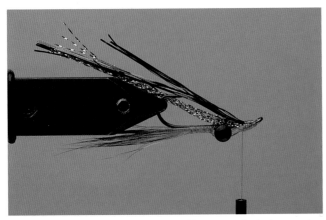

13. Tie in six to eight strands of bronze Flashabou using the fold-in method. Grasp both the gold Krystal Flash and the bronze Flashabou between your thumb and forefinger, and lift up the strand as you wrap the thread back to a point halfway between the metallic eyes and the hook eye.

14. Select a clump of guard hairs from the red fox tail with black tips, reddish brown centers, and grayish butts.

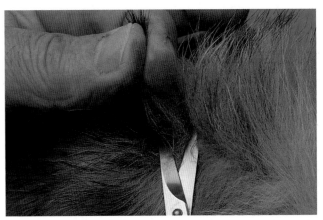

15. Cut the clump of guard hairs and underfur from the skin. Clean out all the underfur from the clump, leaving only the black-tipped guard hairs.

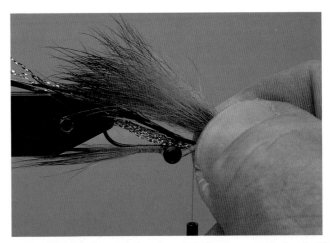

16. Measure the red fox guard hairs to one and a half times the hook shank length.

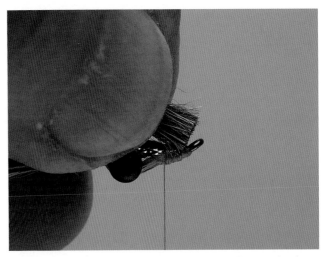

17. Cut the clump to the proper size, and trim the butts evenly. Hold the butts at an angle so that they touch behind the hook eye.

18. With a gathering wrap, position the guard hair clump on top of the hook shank. Grasping the clump of guard hairs, lift up as you wrap down the clump. As you wrap forward, add pressure to the thread, tightening down the butts. Form a neat, tapered head, and whip-finish.

19. Coat the eyes and thread wraps with epoxy or head cement.

CHAPTER 9

Purple Darter

Freshwater darters are an overlooked and under-imitated baitfish species. As a group, the darters are the most colorful of the freshwater baitfish species, and the males in their brilliant spawning colors rival any aquarium fish. Darters are members of the perch family. According to *The American Darters*, more than 140 species dwell in the waters of North America. They are not found in the extreme northeastern United States, eastern Canada, and the waters west of the Continental Divide except where they have been introduced. Pennsylvania has at least twenty-one species.

The presence of darters reflects good water quality and diverse habitat. They prey on insects and small crustaceans, and in turn are eaten by trout, smallmouth bass, walleye, and other fish. Although many of the darters found in Pennsylvania waters are 1 to 2 inches long, two species reach $6^1/2$ inches or more, so it pays to carry several sizes of imitations.

Darters are middepth and bottom dwellers that forage for food on the stream bottom. Many darters do not have swim bladders, buoyant sacs found in many fish that help them float. This lack of buoyancy helps darters stay near the bottom of the stream, as does the water rushing over their flattened, downward-sloping heads. Midwater darter species, such as the blackside darter, have swim bladders that allow them to remain suspended in the water column.

Darters spawn in spring and summer, and spawning can occur for a period of several months. It is during this time that they are most brilliantly colored.

Excited by the encouragement of biologists who regularly study the species, as well as a superb pamphlet called *Dynamic Darters* by Andrew Shiels (distributed by the Pennsylvania Fish and Boat Commission), my son, Bob Jr., and I went to work on fly patterns to represent this important but overlooked baitfish. Bob Jr. noticed

that the darter's two dominant dorsal fins and wide pectoral fins create a broader and wider silhouette, unlike the slim profile of other minnows represented by the Clouser Deep Minnow. He found that calf tail was ideal for creating a bulkier fly. Calf-tail hair has a higher density of fibers than deer tail, and it maintains a robust form

I tie most of my darters with a predominant olive color and multicolored Flashabou hanging from the rear. From top to bottom: Purple Darter, Smoky Gray Darter, Sunburst Darter, Perch Darter, Frog Darter.

Clouser Minnows such as the Foxee Redd Minnow, Purple Darter, and Clouser Deep Minnow imitate baitfish that larger trout feed on. BOB CLOUSER PHOTO

when underwater. We also add a clump of calf tail to the rear of the hook to create a bulkier, broader form. Let the flash materials extend out of and beyond the calf-tail fibers by at least 1 inch. Not only does this flash accent the color of the fly, but the longer flash materials hanging out the back enhance the darting motion of the fly when it is retrieved.

You can fish darter imitations with floating, intermediate, or density-compensated full-sinking fly lines. Our best success on the Susquehanna River comes when using a slow-sinking or intermediate line. At times during high water, I use a medium- to fast-sinking density-compensated full-sinking line to get the fly down. I attach the fly to a 4-foot piece of 8- to 12-pound-test monofilament leader.

Although the different species have many color variations, the most productive base color for our fly patterns and for our local fishery, the Susquehanna River, is olive. Our most successful color variation is the Purple Darter.

Purple Darter

Hook:	Size 4 Mustad 3365A, 3366, S71S SS, or Tiemco 811S
Thread:	6/0 olive Uni-Thread
Eyes:	$^6/_{32}$-inch-diameter ($^1/_{30}$-ounce) lead Wapsi Presentation Eyes, painted red with black pupils
Belly:	Olive calf tail
Middle or Tail:	Purple calf tail
Flash:	Purple Flashabou and red Krystal Flash
Back:	Olive calf tail

This pattern may also be made in several other color combinations. The color of the middle section, or tail, is listed first. The belly and the back are both made of the second color. The number corresponds to the manufacturer's system for each flash color specified. All of these patterns use red Krystal Flash.

Olive Darter
Olive/olive with black Flashabou (6912)

Purple Darter
Purple/olive with purple Flashabou (6913)

Blue Darter
Blue/olive with dark blue Flashabou (6910)

Black and Blue Darter
Blue/black with purple chub Flashabou (6920)

Black and Purple Darter
Purple/black with grape Flashabou (6919)

June Bug Darter
Black/black with june bug Flashabou (6926)

Perch Darter
Orange/olive with perch Flashabou (6927)

Sunburst Darter
Yellow/olive with sunburst Flashabou (6928)

Frog Darter
Green/olive with bullfrog Flashabou (6923)

Ocean Darter
Black/olive with ocean green Flashabou (6922)

Smoky Gray Darter
Light blue/gray with fountain blue Flashabou (6921)

Brown and Orange Darter
Orange/dark brown with gold Flashabou (6902)

Brown Darter
Dark brown/dark brown with bronze Flashabou (6917)

Brown and Yellow Darter
Yellow/dark brown with copper Flashabou (6906)

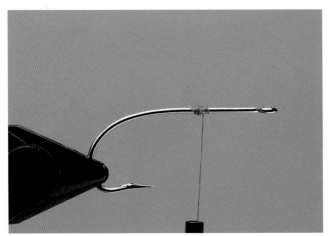

1. Attach the thread at a point one-third the hook shank length in front of the hook eye. Build a thread bump for the metallic eyes.

2. Attach the metallic eyes to the hook shank with cross wraps, and make circle wraps around the base of the cross wraps. Spiral-wrap the thread back to a position above the hook point.

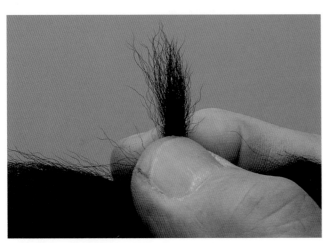

3. Select a bundle of purple calf-tail fibers the thickness of half a pencil.

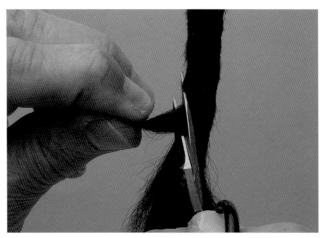

4. Cut the bundle as close to the skin as possible with a pair of sharp scissors.

5. Hold the bundle of fibers between the thumb and forefinger of one hand, and use the other to remove all the short fibers from the bundle and trim the butts evenly.

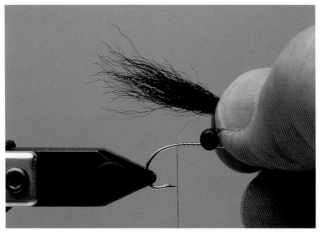

6. Measure the calf-tail bundle so that it is one to one and a half times the length of the hook when tied in.

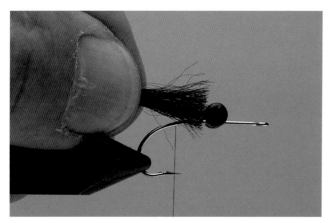

7. Hold the calf-tail fibers against the back of the metallic eyes with one hand, and use the other to begin wrapping around the base of the fibers with a gathering wrap of thread.

8. Continue tightening down on the fibers, and secure them on top of the hook shank. Make sure there is an even thread base from the hook point to the back of the metallic eyes.

9. Bring the thread forward, under the metallic eyes, and take one complete wrap around the hook shank in front of the eyes. Spiral-wrap your thread to just behind the hook eye and back to a point halfway between the hook eye and the metallic eyes.

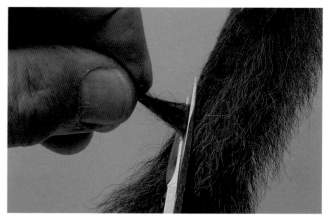

10. Select and cut a bundle of olive calf-tail fibers the same thickness as the purple fibers.

11. Clean out all the short fibers from the butt of the bundle. Trim the butts evenly.

12. Measure the olive calf-tail bundle so that the tips extend to the halfway point of the tied-in purple calf-tail fibers.

13. Hold the olive calf-tail fibers at a 45-degree angle with the butts behind the hook eye. Tie in the butts by making a loose turn of thread over the bundle, continuing to hold the fibers in place.

14. Tighten the gathering wrap by pulling up on the thread, and secure the butts of the calf-tail bundle by wrapping the thread forward to a point behind the eye of the hook. As you wrap the thread forward, continue to lift up on the fibers.

15. Wrap the thread back over the bundle to a point approximately halfway between the hook eye and the metallic eyes.

16. Bring the thread under the metallic eyes and over the bundle of calf-tail fibers with one hand while you hold them with your other hand.

17. Make two loose wraps over the bundle. Push down gently on the thread wraps with the flat side of your scissors tips or your thumb to spread the calf-tail fibers. Secure the positioned fibers behind the metallic eyes.

18. This top view shows how much you should flare the calf-tail fibers. This helps create the chunky profile of the darter. Bring your thread under the metallic eyes to the hook eye, and make one complete turn of thread around the hook shank.

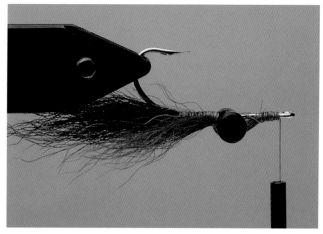

19. Turn the hook over in the vise. Make sure the thread is still positioned behind the hook eye.

20. Using the fold-in method, tie in eight to twelve strands of purple Flashabou at the eye of the hook. Bind down the flash by moving your thread back toward the hook bend with one hand while you lift up the flash with your other hand. Leave the thread at a position halfway between the hook eye and the metallic eyes. Cut the purple Flashabou so it is about two to two and a half times the hook length.

21. With your hands, separate both the long and short strands of Flashabou so that they each are evenly distributed on both sides of the hook. Wrap the thread to behind the hook eye.

22. Tie in four strands of red Krystal Flash.

23. Cut the red Krystal Flash so that it is about as long as the purple Flashabou.

24. Wrap the thread so that it is halfway between the hook eye and the metallic eyes.

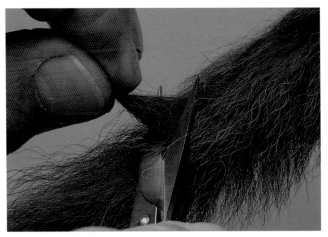

25. Select another bundle of olive calf-tail fibers about half the thickness of a pencil, and cut it from the skin.

26. Remove all the short pieces from the butt end of the bundle. Trim the butts evenly.

27. Measure the length of this bundle to match the length of the other bundle of olive calf-tail fibers.

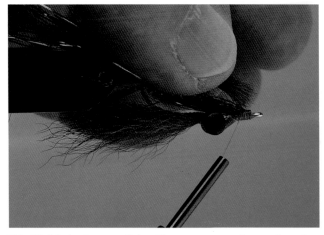

28. Hold the butts of the fibers at an angle so that they are just behind or slightly touching the hook eye.

29. Begin a loose wrap of thread around the butts. Come completely around the bundle, pulling up on the thread as you come around the near side of the hook. Without stopping, continue to wrap down the butts with increasing pressure.

30. Finish securing the olive calf-tail bundle to the hook and form a neat head.

32. Coat the exposed thread and eyes of the completed Purple Darter with epoxy or head cement.

31. Whip-finish the thread.

CHAPTER 10

Clouser Madtom

The origin of the name madtom is unknown. Some say it was given to this baitfish because of its erratic motions; others say it has something to do with its ability to sting. One thing is for sure: Wherever madtoms are found, big bass and trout eat them. In some areas, more big smallmouth are caught on these fish than on any other bait. They are relatively unknown to fly anglers, however, because they are not often seen in streams during the day.

One species in this family of small catfish are called stone cats, a name that reflects their preferred habitat beneath flat rocks in riffles and runs on the riverbed. Various madtom species are distributed widely throughout the United States and Canada. They live in a range of water, from warmwater creeks to rivers as large as the Susquehanna and lower Mississippi.

The stonecat lives in the Ohio River basin and is found throughout the Mississippi River and Great Lakes watersheds. According to the Pennsylvania Fish and Boat Commission, it is not found in Atlantic coast streams south of the Hudson River. In Pennsylvania, this species is the most common one in the western part of the state. In the Susquehanna River, the margined madtom is the most prevalent. Pennsylvania has at least four other species: the rare mountain, brindled, tadpole, and northern madtoms.

Madtoms have poison glands at the base of their pectoral fins, and if you handle them improperly, they can sting you. Like most catfish, madtoms feed at night and eat aquatic insects as well as crayfish and other small invertebrates.

The Clouser Madtom suggests the shape, bulk, and movement of a wide range of immature catfish and madtoms. All of these fish swim along and close to the bottom. They have flat, broad heads similar to those of the sculpins. Their backs are brown, black, olive, or gray, and their bellies are white, tan, or yellow. Effective imitations range from 2 to 6 inches.

To imitate these baitfish, I needed to create a fly that would sink quickly and bounce along the bottom with the hook point up. Flies that ride with the point up hook more fish and are less likely to snag. I wanted a pattern with a catfishlike shape, bulk, and silhouette made from just a few different kinds of materials.

Some of the most effective colors for this pattern are dark brown, rusty brown, olive, black, and gray. Although these are my favorites, sometimes white, yellow, and chartreuse work well. Large trout seem to prefer the subdued shades. My son, Bob Jr., has had great success on the Delaware River enticing large brown trout on the dark brown madtom.

Preparing the materials in advance can save time and helps keep your flies looking consistent. For the Clouser Madtom, I cut the fur strips in advance, taking those for the body from the center or the middle of the back portion of the rabbit hide. This ensures that the fibers are evenly distributed on each side of the strip. Cut the tufts of fur for the pectoral fins from the strips that you removed from the sides of the hide.

In addition to being used as a madtom imitation, the Clouser Madtom is becoming popular in larger sizes for saltwater species. Some anglers have reported great success fishing this fly in the salt, everywhere from New England to Louisiana to Alaska, as a general pattern for fish ranging from cobia to coho.

To fish the Madtom, the fly must be bounced along the bottom or slowly stripped erratically across it. Fish the fly as you would a nymph to bottom-bounce it so that it dead drifts downstream. Cast the fly upstream or slightly across stream and allow it to sink to the bottom.

Watch the drift of the line. Your fly should drift downstream with the speed of the bottom currents. If

Though the Clouser Madtom was designed to imitate baby catfish, it is an excellent imitation in fresh or salt water for a variety of baits. Clockwise from top: black, rusty brown, gray, tan, and olive Clouser Madtoms.

the fly sweeps downstream as fast as the speed of the surface currents, more weight is required to get it down into the slower currents that flow along the bottom. This is where the fly needs to be presented, and it has to flow or tumble along the bottom at the same speed as the bottom currents. If you're not getting the fly to the bottom or achieving a slow downstream bottom bounce, you need to adjust the weight. Add more split-shot to the leader about one foot above the fly. If more are required, place them a foot above each other.

What makes this an effective drift is that the fly tumbles into pockets of slack currents. Most fish hold in these pockets, and any food that washes into them becomes easy pickings for big smallmouth or trout.

In some cases, I use a floating fly line with a 9- to 12-foot leader and make a cast upstream from 20 to 50 feet. I use a tippet up to four feet long at times to get the fly to sink faster and also provide a more drag-free drift. Long casts are important because they allow you to get long drifts with your fly so that you show it to more fish.

To extend the downstream drag-free drift, follow the drift of the fly line where it enters the water with the rod tip, and do not allow the drifting fly line to move ahead of the rod tip. If this occurs, a downstream bow forms, and the water pressure pushing on the bow of the

fly line actually pulls the fly faster than the flow of the bottom currents. This is called drag, and it can occur underwater as well as on the surface.

Sinking-tip or full-sinking fly lines can be very effective when fishing madtom imitations across currents. They are also a great choice when fishing from a drifting boat. In many instances, I prefer a slow-sinking density-compensated full-sinking line for most of my smallmouth fishing on the Susquehanna. This is also my choice when fishing big water for big trout. Sinking-tip lines are another choice when you are fishing over slow-moving currents or shallow water.

I impart action to my madtom imitation by dropping the rod tip to about 6 inches from the water and making short, quick, 1- to 2-foot-long strips with short pauses in between. For this method to be effective, make sure the fly is on or close to the bottom before you retrieve it.

In stillwater, you may need to use a sinking fly line. Allow the fly to sink to or near the bottom, and then pull or crawl it along the bottom. At times, bass or large trout will pick up the fly during pauses in your retrieve. You must be alert and watch the fly line where it enters the water for any movement. In many instances, all you'll feel when a fish picks up the fly is some added weight or resistance when starting the strip after the pause.

Clouser Madtom

Hook:	Size 2 Mustad 3365A, 3366, S71S SS, or Tiemco 811S
Thread:	6/0 dark brown Uni-Thread
Eyes:	$^{6}/_{32}$-inch-diameter ($^{1}/_{30}$-ounce) lead Wapsi Presentation Eyes, painted red with black pupils
Tail:	Rusty brown $^{1}/_{4}$-inch-wide rabbit-fur strip
Pectoral fins:	Rusty brown rabbit fur
Belly:	Dark brown calf-tail fibers
Back:	Dark brown calf-tail fibers
Flash:	Bronze Flashabou

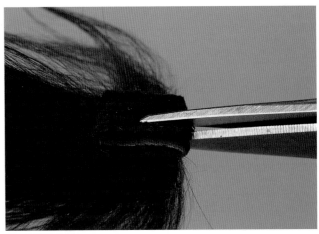

3. Cut a small slot in the middle of the fold with scissors.

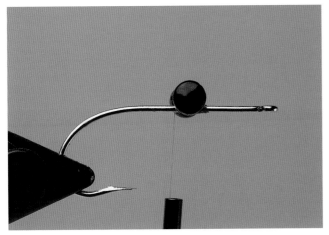

1. Attach the thread at a point one-third the hook shank length in front of the hook eye. Build a thread bump for the metallic eyes. Tie the metallic eyes to the hook shank with cross wraps, and make circle wraps around the base of the cross wraps. Position the thread behind the metallic eyes.

4. Remove the hook from the vise, and insert the point through the slot on the skin side of the rabbit-fur strip.

2. Fold the end of a $^{1}/_{4}$-inch-wide rusty brown rabbit-fur strip back over the fur side of the strip, exposing the skin side.

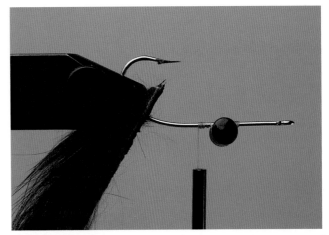

5. Insert the hook back into the vise upside down, and make sure the rabbit strip fibers are on the opposite side from the metallic eyes.

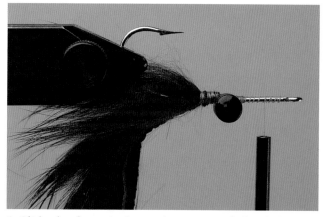

6. Slide the fur strip forward to a point behind the eyes. Bend the skin around the hook with one hand, and use the other to secure the rabbit-fur strip with thread wraps. Move the thread over the metallic eyes to a point halfway between the hook eye and the metallic eyes.

7. Turn the hook so that it is upright, and make sure the thread is still between the hook eye and the metallic eyes.

8. Select a clump of dark brown calf-tail fibers half the thickness of a pencil. Remove all the short fibers from the base of the clump by grasping the top $^1/_4$ inch of the calf-tail hair with the thumb and forefinger of one hand, and pulling the base of the clump with your other hand.

9. Tie the dark brown calf-tail fibers to the hook, first using a gathering wrap, and then making tight turns toward the hook eye.

10. Bring the thread under the metallic eyes with one hand and at the same time, lift up the dark brown calf-tail fibers with the other. Wrap over the fibers in one continual motion while still lifting up on them with your other hand. Make two loose turns of thread, and flare the bundle with your thumb or the flat edge of a scissors blade.

11. This top view shows how much you should flare the fibers. After you flare them, secure the bundle with tight thread wraps.

12. Turn the hook over in the vise. Make one pectoral fin by removing a clump of rabbit fur from the skin about one to one and a quarter times the hook length.

13. Secure the rabbit fur with a pinch wrap on the far side of the hook directly behind the metallic eyes.

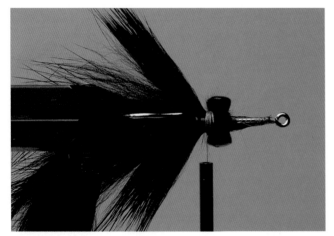

14. Select another clump the same size and length, and secure it to the near side of the hook with a pinch wrap.

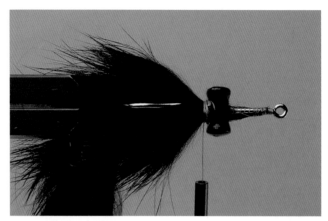

15. Add another clump of the same size and length to the top of the hook shank, and split it with the hook point. You'll be covering up the butts of the rabbit fur, so don't worry too much about covering stray fibers with your thread.

16. Wrap the thread over the metallic eyes to a point halfway between the hook eye and the metallic eyes.

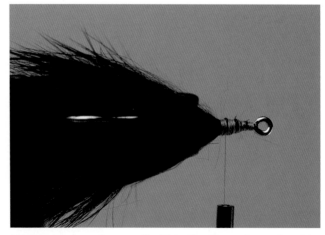

17. Remove a clump of rabbit-fur fibers from the skin, and tie it in on top of the hook shank directly in front of the metallic eyes.

18. Position the thread halfway between the hook eye and the metallic eyes. Select a bundle of calf-tail fibers as long as the hook and half the thickness of a pencil. Prepare the bundle by removing the short hairs from the butt end. Trim the butts evenly.

20. Cover all exposed thread and the eyes of the completed Clouser Madtom with epoxy or head cement.

19. Secure the butts of the calf-tail bundle with a gathering wrap, followed by tight turns toward the hook eye. Form a neat head, and whip-finish. With a single scissors blade, saw the leather side of the fur strip so that it is two times the hook length.

PART III

Subsurface Freshwater Foods

The patterns in this section—the Clouser Crayfish, Swimming Nymph, and Hellgrammite—imitate fish foods that live on the bottom of freshwater rivers and lakes. The nymphs live on the bottom but then travel through the water column to emerge.

Though the dead drift can be a fatal technique for the Deep Minnow, it is often overlooked. I nearly always fish the Hellgrammite and Crayfish dead drift, however, so that the fly bounces along the bottom of the river. The Swimming Nymph is a different story because of the insects it can imitate. One of the most effective techniques for this pattern is to fish the first half or two-thirds of the drift with the fly on the bottom, and then let it swing up in the current at the end of the drift.

These three patterns are heavily weighted with lead or nonlead wire. Without the weight wrapped around the hook, these flies would not perform as well.

PRESENTATION

To dead drift a fly to an upstream target, get in position below and off to the side of the fish or the spot where you think one is. Cast the fly upstream and well above the target so that it has time to sink. After the fly hits the water, drop the rod tip to a few inches above the water and strip in the slack line with your free hand as the fly and line drift down toward you. Be careful not to pull on the fly while stripping in the slack line. Gathering the slack line as the fly drifts toward you allows you to feel the fly tick along the bottom and detect when a fish takes the fly. When you present the fly to a fish across

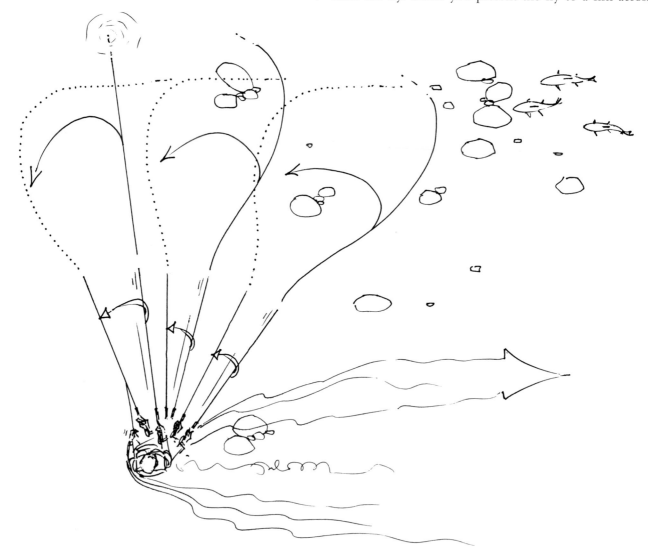

When you cast the fly to a fish across stream from you over various current speeds, an upstream mend counteracts the current's pull on the fly and the fly line. Cast your fly slightly upstream of the fish and throw an upstream mend in the fly line, being careful not to move the fly. This allows your fly to sink. Follow your fly line (where it enters the water) with your rod tip. Make more upstream mends during the drift if the fly line encounters faster moving currents that cause a downstream bow in the line.

stream from you over various current speeds, an upstream mend counteracts the current's pull on the fly and the fly line. Cast your fly slightly upstream of the fish and throw an upstream mend in the fly line, being careful not to move the fly. This allows your fly to sink. Follow your fly line (where it enters the water) with your rod tip. Make more upstream mends during the drift if the fly line encounters faster moving currents that cause a downstream bow in the line. It's important to keep the rod tip moving with the drift of the line so that the line under the rod tip or on the water doesn't get downstream of the rod tip.

Mends help you manage your drift across currents. When you are fishing in faster water or in pockets behind boulders or other structure, you can often get close to the fish and use a technique called high-stick nymphing. The goal here is to keep as much line off the water as possible by raising your arm and rod, or even, at times, just the tip of the rod. Cast upstream and across from your target. Lift as much line off the water as possible to control drag and allow the fly to sink. As the drift continues downstream, keep lifting and follow the line with the rod tip. With short casts and drifts, you only need to lift the rod to control slack; with longer casts and drifts, strip in the slack with your line hand as you raise the rod to keep as much line off the water as possible. To detect strikes, watch the line for any type of unusual movement where it enters the water below the rod tip. As the fly drifts downstream, lower your rod tip to increase the drag-free drift. If you have gathered in slack, let it out as the line drifts downstream.

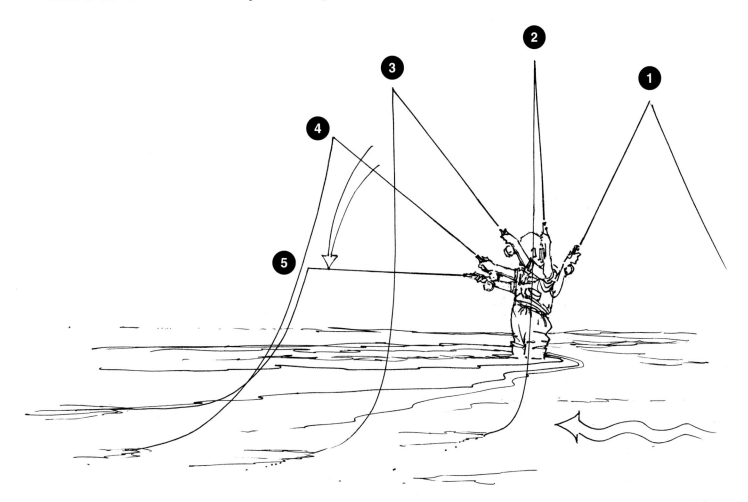

When high-stick nymphing, raise the rod to keep as much line off the water as possible to minimize drag. 1. Cast upstream and lift as much line off the water as possible to control drag and allow the fly to sink. 2. Follow the line with the rod tip as the line, leader, and fly drift downstream. 3. As you follow the drift downstream, lower your rod tip. 4. Continue lowering your rod tip as the fly drifts downstream to extend the drag-free drift. 5. At or near the end of the fly's drag-free drift, your rod tip should be angled downstream with little or no slack in the fly line. As the current pulls the slack out of the fly line, the fly rises toward the surface. You can impart action to the rising fly by lifting the rod tip slowly or twitching it upward. This technique, called the Leisenring Lift, can be effective at times.

The Leisenring Lift is a slight variation of the high-stick technique. At or near the end of the fly's drag-free drift, your rod tip should be angled downstream with little or no slack in the fly line. As the current pulls the slack out of the fly line, the fly rises toward the surface. You can impart action to the rising fly by lifting the rod tip slowly or twitching it upward. This is a deadly technique when used with the Clouser Swimming Nymph.

For a basic dead-drift presentation when you are below the target, cast your fly upstream, drop your rod tip, and strip in line so that it doesn't have a lot of slack and you are tight enough that you can feel the fly tick on the bottom.

To fish a target across stream from you, cast your fly slightly upstream of the target, throw an upstream mend to let your fly sink, and follow it through the drift with your rod tip, throwing upstream mends in your line as necessary to keep the fly on the bottom.

For high-stick nymphing, keep the rod tip and your arm high to keep the line from being affected by the water's pull as you follow the fly through the drift. This technique works best with short casts.

To do the Leisenring Lift, fish the first part of your drift high-sticking, and then drop your rod as the line moves downstream. Let the current swing your fly up through the water column at the end of the drift. This is

CHAPTER 11

Clouser Crayfish

Crayfish are crustaceans that live in many rivers and lakes with semisoft bottoms strewn with rocks, rubble, sunken wood, grass, and other types of structure. They are mainly nocturnal feeders but won't pass up an easy meal during the day.

Water temperatures, day length and sunlight determine activity periods. During winter, crayfish hibernate by burying themselves in silted or muddy bottoms. Many Susquehanna River crayfish winter in slow-water areas under layers of decaying leaves. As water temperatures rise in spring, crayfish prepare to spawn. The female carries an orange egg mass under the abdomen near the tail.

The colors of crayfish vary when they spawn and also differ with their habitat. For instance, crayfish living around grass are greenish olive. I have seen crayfish in variations of blues, grays, dark browns, rust, greens, splotched orange shades, and my favorite color, olive drab. This last shade comes from the general overall army drab color of the silt-covered rocks in the Susquehanna.

Crayfish are available to bass and other fish species from June through October. On the Susquehanna River, they are often so abundant that you can look down a bass's mouth as you are removing a hook and see pincers protruding from the throat. Even though they are available in great numbers, there are certain times of the season when the size of an imitation is important. In early spring, I like smaller imitations. As the summer progresses, the size of the crayfish increases. A variety of imitations from size 4 through 12 might be needed to catch fish, though sizes 4 and 8 account for 99 percent of the fish I catch on the Clouser Crayfish.

I designed the Clouser Crayfish to be fished dead drift along the bottom. Many previous crayfish imitations were tied with buoyant materials and were difficult to bounce along the bottom. The Clouser Crayfish was not designed to be stripped or pulled through the water column. In fact, it loses its effectiveness when fished this way.

The placement of lead wire on each side of the hook shank makes this fly successful during the dead drift. The combination of the lead and other materials allows the crayfish imitation to bounce, rock, roll, and tumble along the bottom, portraying a helpless crayfish. It looks like easy prey to a hungry old smallmouth.

When tying the Clouser Crayfish, various materials can be used for the back cover. I use Furry Foam on hook sizes 4 through 8 and mottled turkey quill segments on size 10. A size 10 with a brown mottled turkey-wing quill is my favorite for trout.

For Clouser Crayfish on hook sizes 4 through 8, I use Furry Foam for the back; for size 10 patterns, I use mottled turkey quill segments. A size 10 with a brown mottled turkey wing quill is my favorite for trout.

Clouser Crayfish

Hook:	Size 6 Mustad R74
Thread:	Tan 6/0 Uni-Thread
Weight:	.025-inch-diameter lead wire
Claws:	Hen mallard flank feather
Antennae:	Pheasant-tail fibers
Carapace cover:	Tip from hen mallard flank feather
Back:	Olive-drab Furry Foam
Underbody:	Pale green dubbing
Legs:	Bleached grizzly, honey dun, or ginger saddle hackles

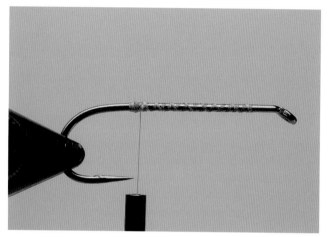

1. Attach the thread above the hook point, and spiral-wrap it to one eye length behind the hook eye. Continue to spiral-wrap the thread back to the hook point. This forms a base for the .030-inch-diameter lead or lead-alternative wire.

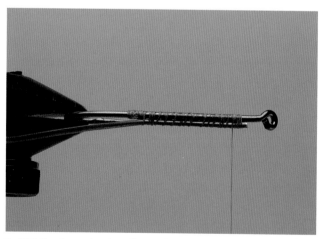

2. While the wire is still on the spool or card it came on, position it on the near side of the hook, making sure the forward end of the lead wire is one eye length behind the hook eye. Wrap your thread to the end of the wire near the hook eye, and take three or four turns at the same spot.

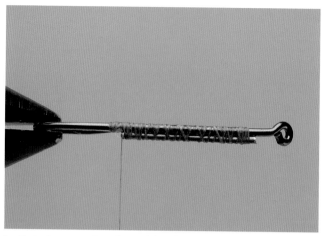

3. Spiral-wrap the thread back to a position just above the hook point. Break off the wire by moving it back and forth, pinch it off with your fingernails, or cut it with the back of your scissors blades (never use the tips).

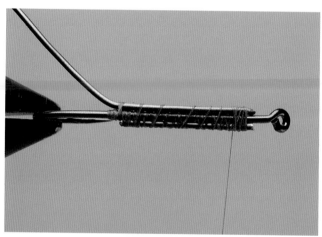

4. Place another section of weighted wire on the far side of the hook shank, making sure the forward end is even with the end of the wire already tied in. Spiral-wrap the thread forward to the ends of both pieces of wire, and make three to four turns with the thread to secure both ends.

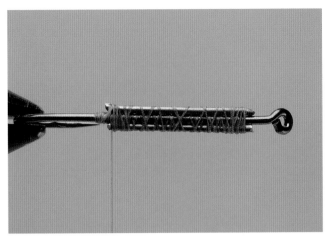

5. Spiral-wrap the thread back to the position above the hook point, and make three to four turns around both pieces of weighted wire. Remove the remaining section of wire that is not tied down.

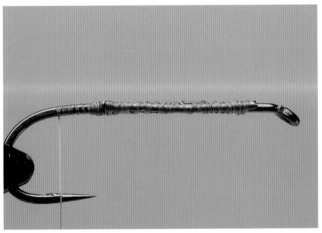

6. Move the thread back to a position above the hook barb.

7. Select six to eight fibers from the side of a male pheasant center tail, and cut them with your scissors.

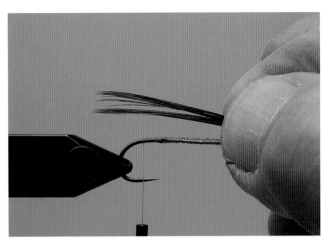

8. Measure the fibers so they are one and a quarter to one and a half the length of the hook.

9. Tie down the butt ends of the pheasant-tail fibers on the hook shank above the point. Wrap forward and back slightly, but do not go onto the bend of the hook. Lift the fibers as you wrap back.

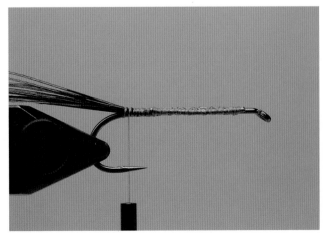

10. Move the thread to a point on the hook shank above the barb.

11. Select a hen mallard flank feather with barbules at least one and a quarter to one and a half times the hook length. Prepare it by holding the tips of the feather with one hand and stroking back the remaining barbules with your other hand.

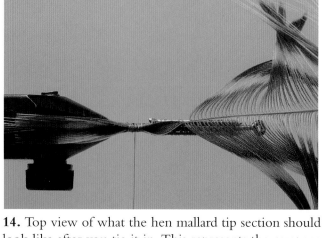

14. Top view of what the hen mallard tip section should look like after you tie it in. This represents the carapace of the crayfish. I'm not sure this step makes a difference to the fish, but I do it anyway—it looks good and uses the tip of the hen mallard feather.

12. Lay the tip of the hen mallard flank feather on top of the pheasant-tail barbules, making sure the length of the hen mallard tip is half that of the pheasant tail.

15. Lift up the hen mallard flank feather, and cut the stem with scissors.

13. Tie down the hen mallard tip on top of the pheasant-tail barbules. After you tie down the hen mallard tip, move the thread to a position above the barb.

16. Save the feather to use later to form the claws.

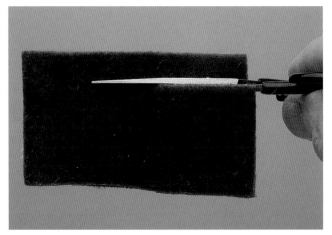

17. Cut a strip of Furry Foam one and a quarter the width of the hook gap.

18. This photo shows the proper width of Furry Foam to use for the back of the Clouser Crayfish.

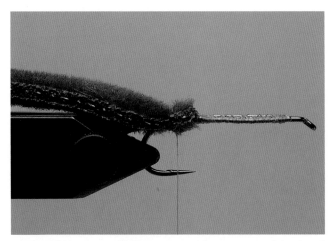

19. Hold the strip of Furry Foam flat on top of the hook shank, and make a loose gathering wrap around it. Tighten the Furry Foam to the shank after you've brought the thread around the shank by pulling up on it.

20. When the Furry Foam is tied properly to the hook shank, it sits centered on top of the shank with the sides curling slightly around it.

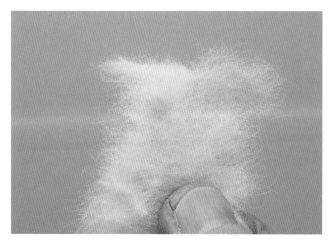

21. Select a small amount of dubbing for the body.

22. Twist the dubbing onto the thread. Apply a small amount of dubbing wax to your forefinger, and roll it between your forefinger, thumb, and thread by pushing the thumb away from you.

23. Form at least a 2-inch-long section of dubbing. If you need more dubbing, add more to complete the next step. Do not try to put too much dubbing on at one time. If you want to build bulk quickly, twist a small amount of dubbing onto the thread, and then twist another bunch of dubbing on top of that.

24. Form the beginning of the underbody of the crayfish by spiral-wrapping the thread forward, covering about one-third of the hook shank with dubbing.

25. With the thumb and forefinger of one hand, grab the hen mallard flank feather that you set aside by the butt of the stem. Use your other thumb and forefinger to stroke about ¹/₂ inch of the barbules forward.

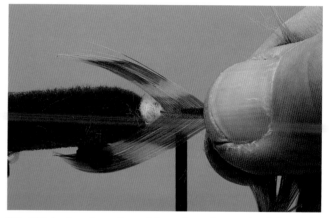

26. With the thread positioned at the end of the dubbing, place the prepared hen mallard feather on top of the dubbing so that the center of the V or the stem of the feather is on the midportion of the dubbed head.

27. Take a loose wrap around the hen mallard barbules and stem, and when it is centered on top of the hook, tie it down. Use your hands to help the thread wrap around the feather so that it cradles the dubbing.

28. Cut the feather.

29. Using the same hen mallard flank feather, pull about ¹/₂ inch of barbules forward.

30. Position the thread against the dubbing, and place the prepared section of feather on top of the tied-in piece. Tie the stem and barbules down over the other portion of hen mallard flank feather.

31. The stacked barbules create the illusion of claws.

32. Cut off the remaining hen mallard flank feather. You can add another layer of fibers if you wish, but two is sufficient for fishing.

33. Twist 1 inch of pale green dubbing onto the thread.

34. Wrap the dubbing tight against the tied-down hen mallard flank feather.

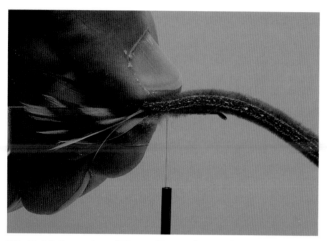

35. Fold the strip of Furry Foam forward over the ball of dubbing and between the claws created by the hen mallard flank feather. Make a loose wrap completely around the foam, and tighten by pulling the bobbin and thread toward you.

36. Form a small neck by wrapping the thread first toward the hook eye, and then back to the rear of the head. Position the thread at the point where you first tied down the Furry Foam.

37. Fold the Furry Foam back over the head, and tie it down. Make sure the tie-down point is on the head side of the small neck formed in the previous step.

38. Top view of the tied-down Furry Foam. The grooved section formed by the doubled-back strip provides a platform on which to tie the saddle hackle in the next step.

39. Select a bleached grizzly or ginger saddle hackle with barbules that extend one and a half times the width of the hook gap.

40. Cut the saddle hackle barbules from the butt end of the stem, leaving ¹/₈ inch of barbule butts on one side of the stem. This helps prevent the stem from pulling out from under the thread. Secure the saddle hackle in the grooved section of the Furry Foam.

41. Wrap the thread forward over the saddle hackle stem toward the hook eye.

42. Fold back the remaining section of saddle hackle stem and wrap the thread over the folded stem. This helps lock in the feather.

43. Wrap the thread forward so that it is in front of the weighted wire.

44. Twist more pale green dubbing onto your thread, about 3 inches. Wrap the thread back to the base of the head and slightly over the saddle hackle. Let the bobbin hang at this point.

45. Wrap the saddle hackle forward with hackle pliers, and make one full turn of the hackle at the base of the Furry Foam. Make sure the bobbin remains in this position while you are wrapping the hackle forward.

46. Make three spiral wraps with the saddle hackle, ending just at the rear of the weighted wire, but not off of it. Do not tie off or wrap the hackle on the hook shank.

47. Leave the hackle pliers attached to the tip section of the saddle hackle. Wrap the thread about one-third the length of the dubbed body toward the hook eye.

48. Fold the Furry Foam forward, and make one full loose turn with the thread around the foam and body. Pull the thread toward you to tighten the segment, as in the next photo. Make another full turn of the thread over the previous one to secure the wrap.

49. The first completed segment of the back of the Clouser Crayfish.

50. Fold the Furry Foam back, and move the thread forward half the distance of the remaining dubbed portion of the body.

51. Fold the Furry Foam forward, and make one full loose turn around it and the body. Tighten by pulling the thread toward you. Make another tight turn with the thread over the previous wrap to secure the segment.

52. The second completed segment of the back of the Clouser Crayfish.

53. Fold the Furry Foam back over the body, wrap the thread forward through the saddle hackle, and make one

full turn around the dubbed body at a position near the end of the lead that forms the flat underbody. Keep the thread on the lead when you tighten down the segments. Do not tighten the last segment on the hook shank.

54. Fold the Furry Foam forward, and make a full loose wrap around it and the body. Pull the thread toward you to secure the last segment.

55. The final segment in the back of the Clouser Crayfish.

56. Cut the remaining saddle hackle.

59. Fold the Furry Foam over the hook eye, and force the eye through the foam.

57. Fold the Furry Foam back, and form a thread foundation on the bare hook shank.

60. You can make a small cut to help the hook eye go through the Furry Foam.

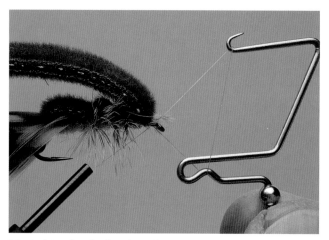

58. Whip-finish the thread.

61. Trim the Furry Foam about $1/4$ inch below the hook eye.

CLOUSER CRAYFISH ■ 103

62. Round off the corners of the Furry Foam strip with your scissors so it looks like a crayfish tail.

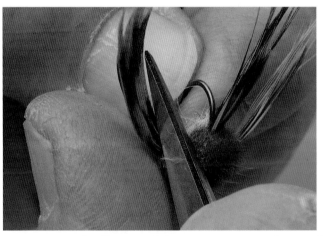

63. To create the illusion of claws, position one clump of the hen mallard flank barbules against your thumb, and place the back edge of the scissors against the clump. Squeezing lightly, pull the scissors up, scraping the barbules as though you were curling a ribbon on a gift.

64. If done properly, the clump of hen mallard barbules will curl.

65. Curl the other claws using the same procedure.

66. A bottom view of the Clouser Crayfish. Add a little head cement to the thread wraps at the hook eye.

CHAPTER 12

Clouser Hellgrammite

Hellgrammites are an important year-round food source for bass and trout, especially so in spring and early summer. The ugly hellgrammites are most active at this time of the year, as they crawl from their nymphal habitat in fast-moving riffle water to the streambank, where they eventually mature into the equally homely dobsonflies. During this precarious trip, many hellgrammites are swept off the river bottom and drift helplessly in the currents. Fish key on these insects during this migration and drift.

The hellgrammite is the larval stage of the dobsonfly, a large, winged insect that emerges around dusk through the summer on many streams across the United States. While some fish feed on the winged adults, they gorge on the nymphal form.

These creatures live in a wide variety of habitats, from small streams to stillwater, but they generally prefer cool rivers with good-quality, highly oxygenated water. They spend their nymphal stage living under rocks and prey on a wide range of other aquatic insects, such as mayfly, caddis, and stonefly nymphs. Hellgrammites average 2 to 3 inches long, though they can grow up to 5 inches. Their mandibles, or pincers, help them catch and eat aquatic insects.

The nymphal stage lasts an average of one to three years, and then, usually in spring or summer, the nymph crawls out of the water to find a suitable place to dig a hole and emerge. It digs underground or burrows under leaves, where it pupates and emerges as an adult a few weeks later.

Hellgrammites are usually on the move from late May until mid-July. In rivers where hellgrammites live, bass and trout show a strong preference for $1/4$- to 3-inch-long brown and black nymphs. On Pennsylvania's lower Susquehanna River in the Harrisburg area, the first three weeks in June are best for hellgrammite fishing, but

Clouser Hellgrammite patterns fish extremely well all summer.

The nymphal hellgrammites cling to the bottom of stones. You can scout rivers for these large insects by wading and flipping over flat stones in freestone streams. Beware of the pincers at the head, which can nip your fingers. The best way to grab a hellgrammite is like a snake—behind the back of the head.

Two presentations work best with the Clouser Hellgrammite: dead drift in fast water and side swimming in side pools and slicks.

To present your fly dead drift, cast a weighted pattern upstream. Provide enough slack to allow the nymph

Trout gorge on hellgrammites, the nymphal form of the dobsonfly, spring, summer, and fall. Dead drift a Clouser Hellgrammite through the riffles or heads of pools, or swim it through slow water. BOB CLOUSER PHOTO

to drift freely downstream. This pattern drifts best when fished on a tippet 24 to 36 inches long. As with any nymph, when you see a hesitation in the drift or feel a tap, set the hook. A strike indicator helps you visually detect even the softest take.

Use a lightly weighted pattern for the side-swimming technique in pools off the main current and in long, slow slicks. Cast the nymph quartering across and upstream. Lift the rod tip while stripping line to swim the fly properly in these slower waters.

Clouser Hellgrammite, Olive (shown in steps)

Thread:	6/0 black Uni-Thread
Hook:	Size 4 Mustad 3365A, 3366, S71S SS, or Tiemco 811S
Weight:	.020-inch- or .025-inch-diameter lead wire
Tail:	Olive rabbit-fur strip
Body:	Olive rabbit fur in dubbing loop
Legs:	Grizzly hackle
Overbody:	Brown Furry Foam

Clouser Hellgrammite, Black

Thread:	6/0 black Uni-Thread
Hook:	Size 4 Mustad 3365A, 3366, S71S SS, or Tiemco 811S
Weight:	.020-inch- or .025-inch-diameter lead wire
Tail:	Black marabou or rabbit-fur strip
Body:	Black rabbit fur in dubbing loop
Legs:	Grizzly hackle
Overbody:	Black Furry Foam

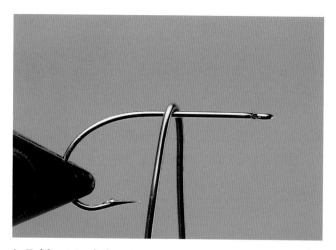

1. Fold a 6-inch-long section of .030-inch-diameter lead or lead-alternative wire over the hook, making sure the rear tag end is shorter than the main forward piece (about 1 inch long).

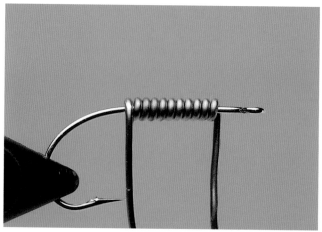

2. Hold the short tag end with the forefinger and thumb of one hand, grasp the long forward section with the forefinger and thumb of your other, and wind the weighted wire forward ten to twelve turns.

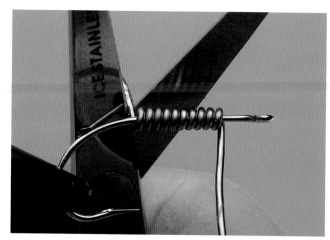

3. Snip away both tag ends of excess wire with the back of your scissors blades.

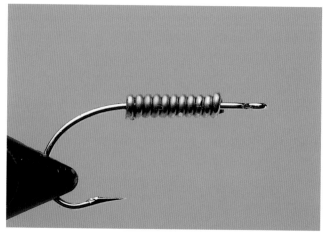

4. Position the wire so the rear portion is above the hook point and the forward portion is at least one hook eye length behind the eye.

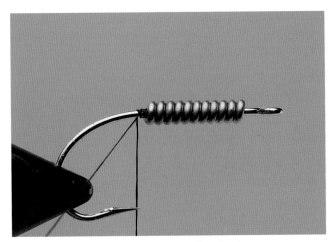

5. Attach thread behind the weighted wire.

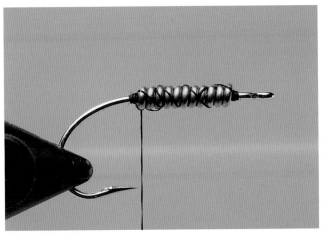

6. Tie down the wire by spiral-wrapping forward through it to the far end. Wrap the tying around the hook shank two to three turns, and spiral-wrap it back to the rear of the wire coils. This helps keep the wire in position when you tie materials over it.

7. Select a clump of rabbit fur approximately the full length of the hook, and remove it from the skin.

8. Trim the butts of the rabbit-fur clump evenly, and tie down the clump onto the hook shank behind the wire. If you hold the fur on the near side of the clump at an angle when you tie it in, thread torque pulls it on top of the shank.

9. The rabbit fur should be centered on top of the hook.

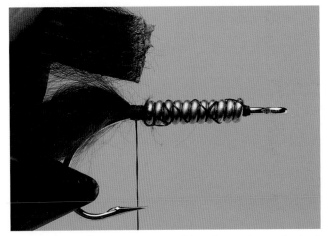

10. Select a $\frac{1}{4}$-inch-wide rabbit-fur strip, and tie it down on top of the rabbit-fur clump.

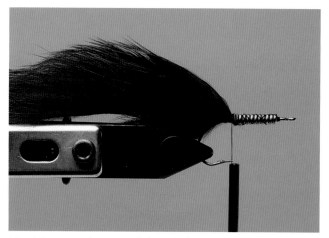

11. After you have tied down the rabbit-fur strip, position the thread in front of the hook point for the next step.

12. From the rabbit strip or skin, remove a clump of rabbit fur approximately the length of the hook.

13. Tie the rabbit-fur clump on top of the rabbit-fur strip. The clump should be tied down directly behind the lead coils, and the remaining butts of the clump are tied down on top of the lead coils. Position the thread forward of the hook point.

14. Prepare a strip of Furry Foam 3 to 4 inches long and the width of one and a half times the hook gap in width.

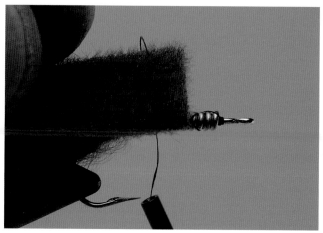

15. Place the end of the Furry Foam flat on top of the weighted wire coils, and make a loose wrap, bringing the thread to a position between you and the edge of the foam strip.

16. Pull the thread toward you to tighten the Furry Foam to the hook.

17. Secure the rabbit-fur strip by wrapping the thread forward to the end of the Furry Foam and then back to the starting point.

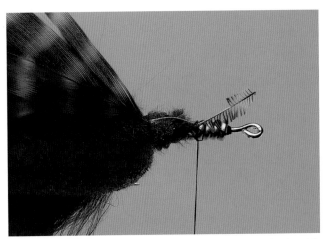

19. Tie down the stem of the grizzly saddle hackle behind the Furry Foam strip. Wrap the thread forward over the hackle stem to a point halfway along the wire.

18. Select a grizzly saddle hackle with barbules one and a half to one and three-fourths the width of the hook gap. Strip or cut all the barbules from one side, and cut the other side to leave a small amount of barbules.

20. Fold the end of the hackle stem back, and wrap the thread over it.

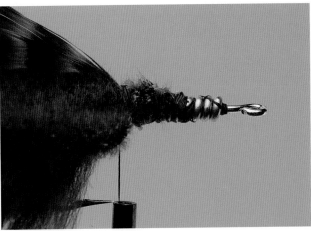

21. Make sure the thread is above the hook point after you bind down the hackle stem.

22. Form a dubbing loop, and insert a clump of rabbit fur cut from the hide into the loop. Pull both sides of the loop tight. Spread out the rabbit fur in the center of the loop so you have at least $1^1/_2$ to 2 inches of fibers in the loop.

23. Spin the dubbing loop until all the rabbit hair in the loop looks like a bottle brush.

24. Wrap the flared rabbit-fur loop forward, forming a hair body.

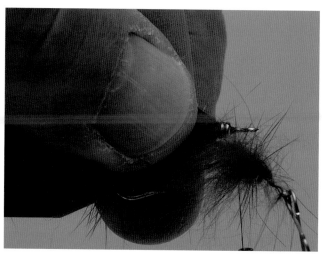

25. As you wrap each turn of the flared rabbit hair in the loop, tease or pull the fibers back with your left thumb and forefinger.

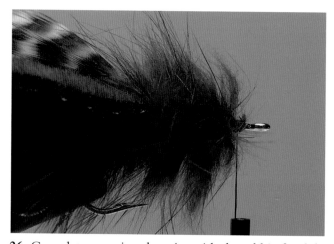

26. Complete covering the wire with the rabbit-fur dubbing loop, and tie it off one eye length behind the hook eye.

27. Attach a pair of hackle pliers to the tip section of the grizzly hackle, and wind the hackle through the rabbit hairs. Stop wrapping when you reach one eye length behind the hook eye.

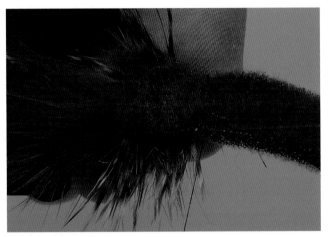

28. Fold the Furry Foam forward over the top of the body, spreading out the rabbit-fur fibers and the grizzly hackle as you press the strip down on top of the body.

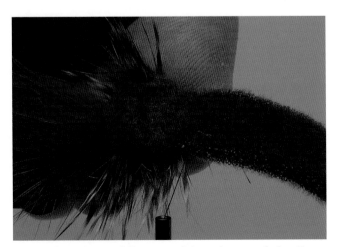

29. Make a loose full turn of thread around the Furry Foam and hook shank.

30. Pull the thread toward you as you tighten it.

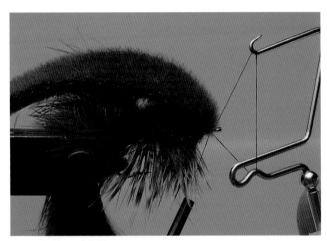

31. Fold the Furry Foam back over the body, form a neat head with the thread, and whip-finish.

32. Saw the skin of the rabbit-fur strip 2 inches from the rear of the fly with one scissors blade.

33. The long rabbit-strip tail undulates in the water. You can vary the length depending on the naturals in your area and your personal preference for casting and fishing.

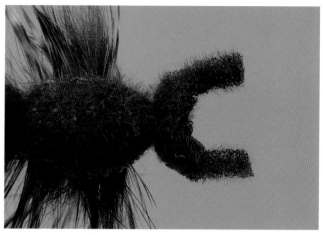

36. Cut out a diamond-shaped section from the Furry Foam to form the pincers.

34. Cut the Furry Foam straight, $^3/_8$ inch in front of the fly.

37. Add head cement to the eye of the finished Clouser Hellgrammite. This pattern is effective in brown, black, and olive.

35. Trim each corner off the head so that the Furry Foam looks like an arrowhead.

CHAPTER 13

Clouser Swimming Nymph

Many rivers and lakes across the country have populations of damselflies, dragonflies, mayflies, and stoneflies. The nymphal forms of many of these aquatic insects are large. They swim the surface of the water, then crawl across rocks in the stream or up on the banks to emerge. Many species of mayfly nymphs, such as yellow, green, and brown drakes, large *Isonychia,* or *Hexagenia limbata* (Hex), swim in an undulating motion when they begin to emerge.

Before developing the Swimming Nymph, I read Gary Borger's book *Nymphs.* One pattern had a rabbit-fur strip attached to the rear of the abdomen. I liked the idea of a soft material used as a tail and extension of an abdomen. At that time, I had no rabbit-fur strips, so I substituted marabou that I had on hand. Using Gary's style of attaching soft materials to the rear of nymphs, I designed a swimming nymph for the Susquehanna River's smallmouth bass.

I wanted to build into the Swimming Nymph both a robust shape and the swimming motion the naturals use to move through the water. From experience, I knew that a key factor was the amount of weight and its placement in the fly. The swimming nymph needed to be heavy to be fished properly and effectively. The naturals that I had observed moved along the bottom during their journey toward emergence.

Covering the entire shank with lead wire, and then adding another layer over the top on just the forward half of the shank created the form of a nymph, with a thin abdomen and a robust thorax. The forward placement of the heaviest section of weight would cause the marabou tail to move and undulate when fished with a short, jerky, speed-up-and-stop stripping retrieve. With soft tail material, such as marabou or rabbit fur, even when dead drifting a fly, a slight shake of the rod tip adds motion to

the rear portion. The soft materials on the fly move from the bouncing motion of the weight alone.

Generally, colors should closely match the natural you are imitating. Insects tend to adopt the coloration of the habitat in which they live. Many large swimming-type nymphs burrow into mud-silted bottoms. During emergence, as the silt washes from their bodies, their true colors are revealed. Effective colors for the Susquehanna

The Swimming Nymph is effective anywhere fish feed on damselflies or large mayfly nymphs that swim to the banks or surface of the water to hatch. Small Swimming Nymphs, with or without the bead, work well for trout. Here, Linda Heller releases a trout on the Yampa River, Colorado.

BOB CLOUSER PHOTO

These rusty brown and dirty yellow Swimming Nymphs are tied with rabbit-fur and marabou tails. In versions of this fly tied without a bead, I like to use a bright red or rusty orange thread head (top).

are rusty brown, dirty yellow, and gray. In general, these colors will work in most streams and stillwater across the country. I use dirty yellow to match many of the damselfly nymphs found in the area where I fish. Dark gray to dark olive can be used if dragonfly nymphs are prevalent.

Although this pattern is effective throughout the water column, I catch most of my fish by using the Clouser Swimming Nymph along the bottom. Various techniques can be used with this pattern, but I prefer to fish it across and downstream with a slow strip or crawl across the bottom. When wade-fishing, search for a pool with slow-moving water current, and cast slightly up and across stream. When fishing from a drifting boat, cast toward the shoreline and drop your rod tip to about six inches from the surface. In either case, allow the fly to sink to the bottom, and retrieve it with short, slow strips, which activate the marabou or rabbit-fur tail. Strikes from bass or trout are easy to detect when using this type of retrieve; you may feel a jolt or just the weight from the take.

This pattern is also effective when fish are rising to emerging insects. Cast the fly just above the ring of the riseform, and retrieve it before it has a chance to sink. Be alert and ready to strike, because a bass will take the fly as soon as it hits the water.

The Clouser Swimming Nymph has become a mainstay in many anglers' fly boxes. It has proven a favorite for carp, trout, smallmouth, and other species. I like to use hook sizes 6 and 8 for bass and sizes 10 and 12 for trout. This pattern can be tied with a variety of materials. I prefer to use either rabbit fur or marabou for the tail, peacock strands for the wing-case cover, hen hackle for the legs, and a sparkle-type dubbing for the body. The fly can be tied with or without beads. Estaz can be used to form the thorax in place of the dubbing; I call this fly the Sparkle Belly Swimming Nymph.

Clouser Swimming Nymph	
Hook:	Size 8 Mustad R74
Bead:	3/16-inch-diameter gold bead
Weight:	.020-inch-diameter lead wire
Thread:	6/0 fire orange Uni-Thread
Tail:	Dark brown marabou and bronze Flashabou
Body:	Dark rusty dubbing
Wingcase:	Peacock herl from eye
Legs:	Speckled brown hen-back feather

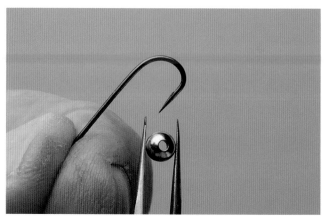

1. Insert the point of the hook through the smaller hole of a 3/16-inch-diameter gold bead.

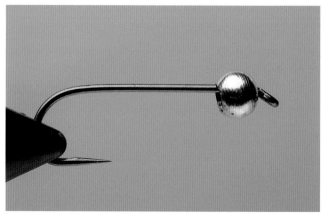

2. Slide the bead over the hook shank, position it behind the hook eye, and insert the hook into the vise.

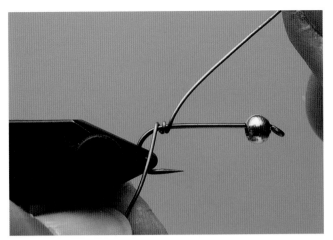

3. Attach an 8-inch piece of .025-inch-diameter lead or lead-alternative wire at the rear of the hook shank.

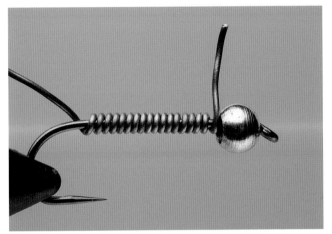

4. Wrap the lead wire forward, making sixteen full turns, ending behind the bead.

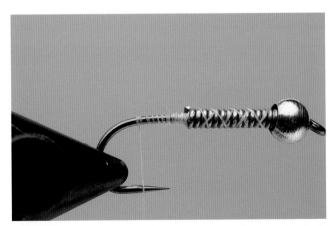

5. Insert the forward end of the wire coils into the hole in the bead. Attach the thread at the end of the hook behind the wire wraps. Wrap the thread forward and back through the wire. Make a few turns of thread behind the wire coils, securing the wire into position. Position the thread above the hook barb.

6. Measure a rusty brown marabou blood quill so it is two times the length of the hook, and trim the butts evenly.

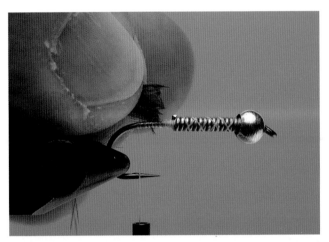

7. Position the marabou butts on top of the hook shank behind the wire coils.

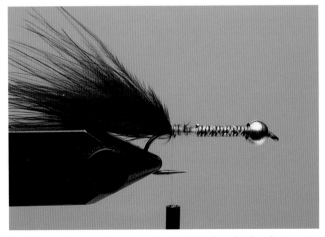

8. Tie in the marabou on top of the hook shank.

9. Tie in six to eight strands of bronze Flashabou by using the fold-in method at the point where the marabou is secured, and cut it so that it is one and a half times the length of the marabou.

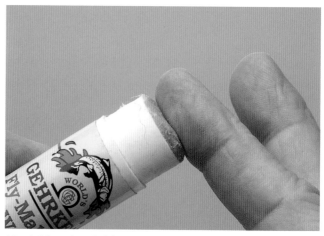

12. Add tacky dubbing wax onto the forefinger of your right hand until the thumb and forefinger stick together lightly.

10. Select another rusty brown marabou blood quill, and measure to the length of the marabou already on the hook.

13. Touch a small amount of rusty brown dubbing to the waxed section of the forefinger, and place the thread over the dubbing as shown above.

11. Tie the marabou blood quill on top of the bronze Flashabou.

14. Twist the dubbing onto the thread by squeezing the dubbing and thread while at the same time rolling the dubbing onto the thread.

15. Wrap the dubbed thread around the hook shank to a point just behind the wraps of wire.

16. Select a small clump of about twelve to fifteen strands of strung peacock herl, and cut off the tips evenly.

17. Place the tips of the peacock herl on top of the wire wraps.

18. Tie down the tips on top of the wire coils.

19. Select a soft hackle from a brown speckled hen back with barbules two times the width of the hook gap. Remove the soft fibers from the butt of the stem.

20. Hold the tip of the hen back feather, and stroke the fibers back toward the butt of the stem.

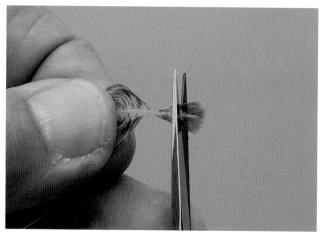

21. Cut off the tip section of the hen back feather so the tips are even.

22. Tie in the hen feather (at the point where you pulled the barbs back) on top of the peacock herl.

23. Bind the tip of the feather to the wire.

24. Add more rusty brown dubbing to the thread, and wrap the dubbing rope forward to a point just behind the bead.

25. Attach a pair of hackle pliers to the butt end of the stem of the hen feather. Sweep the barbs back with your forefinger as you wrap the feather to a point just behind the bead.

26. Tie the butt of the hen feather stem behind the bead with at least four snug turns of thread.

27. Snip the hackle stem after tying off the feather.

28. Fold the clump of peacock herl forward over the top of the fly body.

29. The clump of peacock herl should form a robust wing case.

30. Tie off the peacock herl with four tight turns of thread over the herl directly behind the bead.

31. Top view.

32. Lift the clump of peacock herl, and move the thread in front of the clump.

33. Make four snug turns with the thread behind the bead, and whip-finish.

35. The butts extending over the bead add bulk to the nymph.

34. Trim the clump of peacock herl.

PART IV

Surface Flies

Casting a surface fly and watching the take, whether it's a busting strike or a simple gentle sip, always gives me goosebumps. I start using surface flies on the Susquehanna when the fish begin looking to the surface, around when the caddis start hatching in June, and then when the whiteflies start hatching around the end of July. Early August through November typically is prime surface time. The less speed and the clearer the water, the more effective these flies are. On a nice sunny day when there is enough clarity that shadows are created on the bottom, I think fish are drawn by shadows from things on the surface and come up to take a look.

Generally speaking, there are four categories of surface flies for which I have patterns. The first is poppers, such as the EZ Popper, which are designed to create a lot of commotion on the surface and draw strikes from fish attracted to that action. They are best used when fish are aggressive and not easily scared by the noise of the popper.

The second category is diving-type surface patterns, such as the Suspender and Crippled Minnow, which may be viewed like emergers in the aquatic insect world. These patterns hang well below the surface, as in the case of the Suspender, or just below it, as in the case of the Crippled Minnow, and are good alternatives to try when fish won't commit to the popper or are spooked by it.

The third category, and the one that I fish most often these days, consists of Floating Minnows and Bright Sides Minnows. These are like sliders in that they move across the surface with little disturbance. The Floating Minnow also hangs a bit in the water like the Crippled Minnow. These flies present a more realistic profile to fish then poppers do, and they don't create much disturbance when retrieved, making them my choice for spooky fish.

The fourth category consists of large mayfly adult patterns such as the Clouser Green Drake Dun. For those times when fish are keying in on surface insects, I tie a basic, heavily hackled dry fly that I adapt to imitate local hatches of white flies (*Ephoron leukon*), drakes, and other large mayflies. Many wraps of hackle, which I often trim flat on the bottom of the flat, help the fly float.

CHAPTER 14

Clouser Crippled Minnow

Along with the Clouser Crayfish, the Crippled Minnow was one of my first bass-fly patterns back in the early 1980s. When I designed this fly, I was inspired by Al Troth's bullhead patterns. Many know Troth as the inventor of one of the most popular dry flies ever, the Elk Hair Caddis, but the streamers he designed for Montana trout were well ahead of their time and inspired many, including myself, to learn how to work with deer hair. I copied the head style of some of his deer-hair baitfish patterns. I just trimmed the head differently, with a rounded bottom like a canoe, so that it sits in the film.

I designed this fly to rest on the surface with only a portion of the head above water and dive under the surface when retrieved. The most effective spinning and casting surface lures were always the ones that hung in the surface film with only the head exposed. I wanted this trait in a surface fly. The rear portion of the fly is tied with materials that soak up water, and the front is deer-body hair, which floats. With this combination, the fly hangs in the surface film like a feeding or injured baitfish.

If you trim the bottom of the head flat, the fly doesn't hang in the film, but floats high on the surface. For the fly to sit properly, trim the bottom close to the bottom of the hook shank; the top edges of the round bottom have to be above the hook shank. The top portion of the head can be trimmed in a semioval half the distance of the head's length. The remaining deer-hair fibers on top of the rear portion of the head are trimmed to form a collar similar to that on Dahlberg's Diver. The collar allows the fly to dive and also creates a surface disturbance. When trimming the deer hair, be careful not to take too much off. You can always trim more hair off later, but you cannot put it back.

My favorite color combination is red and white, although Crippled Minnows can be tied in many colors. Sizes 4 and 6 get the most attention from Susquehanna River smallmouth.

The Crippled Minnow fishes better after it becomes waterlogged, and even better once it has caught a few fish and the fish slime pulls the fly down so that it hangs low in or slightly under the surface film. I dress the head on the trimmed portion if I want to fish it high, but it generally sinks only four to six inches undressed.

An effective technique is to fish this fly on intermediate or sinking lines like a Muddler Minnow. When fishing the Crippled Minnow underwater, the quicker you use the Susquehanna Strip, the more erratically it swims. Sometimes that motion is just what is needed to get the fish to hit the fly.

Clouser Crippled Minnow

Hook:	Size 6 Mustad R74
Thread:	6/0 white Uni-Thread for the body; white Danville Flymaster Plus for spinning the deer-hair head
Body:	Peacock herl and white Antron or Sparkle Yarn
Throat:	Red wool or yarn
Tail:	Red over white marabou blood feathers
Flash:	Pearl Flashabou
Head:	Red and white deer-body hair, spun on the hook and trimmed to shape

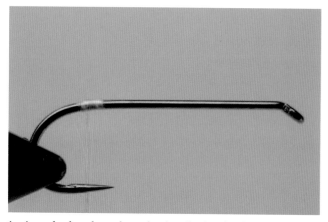

1. Attach the thread to the hook shank above the barb.

2. Select a marabou blood feather at least one and a half times the length of the hook. Cut the butts evenly.

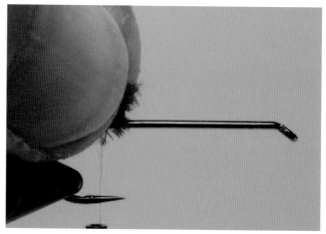

3. Tie down the butts onto the hook shank using a pinch wrap.

4. Position the thread slightly in front of the hook point.

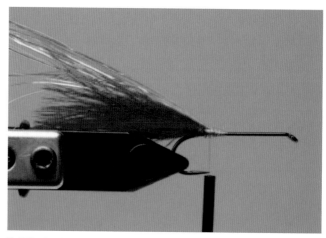

5. Tie in six to ten strands of Flashabou using the fold-in method. Wrap the thread back to a point above the hook point, lifting the Flashabou and marabou as you do so.

6. Select another marabou blood feather the same length as the first one, and trim the butts evenly.

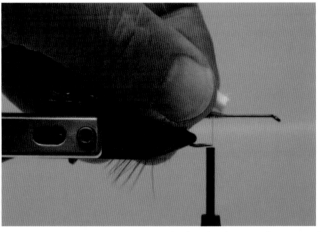

7. Using the pinch wrap, attach the feather to the top of the hook shank and the tied-down Flashabou.

8. Wrap the thread one or two wraps in front of the point of the hook.

9. Select a clump of fifteen to twenty strands of peacock herl, and cut off the tips evenly.

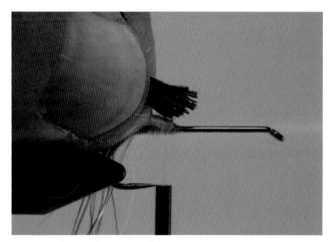

10. Tie down the tips of the peacock herl on top of the marabou feather.

11. Wrap over the peacock herl at the tie-down point, and position the thread at the midpoint of the hook shank.

12. Tie in a 10-inch piece of white sparkle yarn.

13. Tie the yarn down by wrapping the thread toward the rear of the hook to a position on top of the secured peacock herl. Wrap the thread back to the midpoint of the hook shank.

14. Wrap the white sparkle yarn so that each wrap is tight against the previous one to one full turn past the midpoint of the hook. Tie off the white yarn and cut the excess.

15. Move the thread back to the midpoint of the hook shank over the tied-down yarn.

16. Cut a 4-inch section of four-stranded red wool yarn, and separate the strands into two sections.

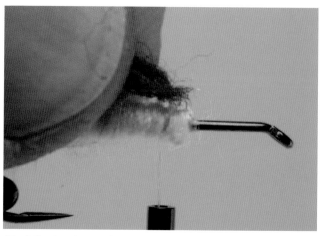

17. Tie in the red wool yarn at the midpoint of the hook shank. Wrap the thread to a point in front of the white yarn.

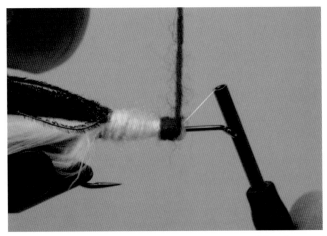

18. Wrap the red yarn forward, and tie it off in front of the white yarn.

19. Trim the tag end of the red yarn, and wrap over any area that you couldn't cut.

20. Pull the peacock herl bundle forward with one hand, keeping it on top of the body.

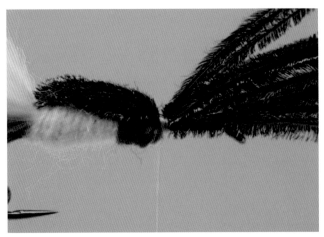

21. With your other hand, tie down the bundle of herl in front of the red yarn. If you are right-handed, pull the herl forward with your right hand, and with your left, bring the bobbin up and around the bundle holding it to the hook shank. You can now let go of the herl with your right hand and use that hand to complete fastening

22. Trim the excess herl and wrap over butts.

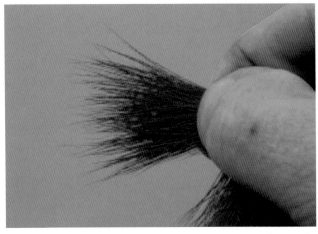

23. Select a clump of red deer-body hair about the thickness of a wooden pencil.

24. Prepare the clump of deer-body hair by removing the short and softer underbody fibers. I use my hands, but you can also use a mustache comb.

25. Measure the fibers for length. The butts will flare and you'll trim those fibers, but you won't trim the tapered ends extending over the back of the fly.

26. Hold the tips of the deer-hair bundle between your thumb and forefinger to prevent the hair from spinning around the hook shank. Make a full loose turn using a

gathering wrap, and pull the thread and bobbin straight up, putting pressure on the thread as you lift. The increasing pressure from the thread as it tightens will cause the hair to flare.

27. Make two more tight turns of thread over the previous wraps to secure the bundle of deer-body hair.

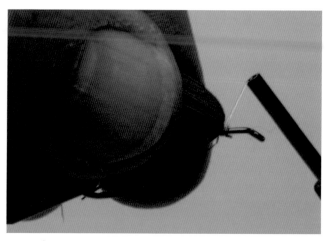

28. Lift as much of the flared butt ends of the deer-hair bundle as you can up and toward the rear of the hook. Make three tight turns of the thread in front of the butts, securing the bundle in place.

29. This is how the first bundle should look after you have tied it in. By holding it when you wrap, you keep most of the hair on top of the hook shank.

30. Select another bundle of deer-body hair and prepare it as you did the last one.

31. Place the deer-hair bundle against the hook shank at almost a right angle, and make two loose wraps around the hook shank and the deer-hair bundle, increasing pressure as you make a full turn around the hook shank.

Let go of the deer-body hair as you wrap around the hook shank so the hair flares and circles the hook shank.

32. This is how the head should look after you spin the second bundle of deer-body hair. Make sure the fibers from the second bundle completely circle the hook.

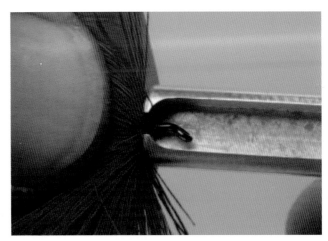

33. Use a hair-packing tool or your fingertips to compact the spun deer hair.

34. After packing the hair, the thread should be one eye length behind the hook eye. If you want to add another bunch of red hair, you can.

35. Select a bundle of white deer-body hair about half the thickness of a wooden pencil, and prepare it like the other deer hair.

36. Hold the white deer-hair bundle alongside of the hook shank, and make two loose wraps around the deer-hair and the hook shank.

37. Let go of the tips of the white deer-hair bundle, and increase pressure on the thread as you wrap over the bundle and around the hook shank. Pull the flared fibers back, and make two tight turns in front of the white bundle of deer-body hair.

38. Pack the white hair.

39. If you have space, select another bundle of white hair and spin it around the hook.

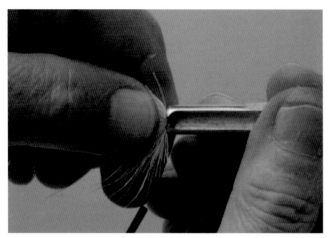

40. Pack all the deer-tail fibers by placing the packing tool in front of the bundle of white deer-body hair and pulling the spun fibers back with your thumb and forefinger. Don't make the head too tight. This fly fishes best if it doesn't float high in the water.

41. Sweep the spun deer-hair fibers back, and wrap a neat thread head.

42. Whip-finish the thread, and take the fly out of the vise to trim it.

43. With a pair of sharp scissors, make the first cut flush along the bottom.

44. The first cut should produce a flat body with about ⅛-inch-long deer-hair fibers protruding from the hook shank.

45. Lay the scissors at an angle on top of the spun deer hair, and cut an upward slant on the top of the deer-hair head. Make sure you cut away only the top white portion of the deer hair.

46. Close-up top view of how the second cut should look.

49. A view of a properly trimmed side.

47. After you have completed trimming the white deer-body hair, trim away about ⅛ inch of the red deer-body hair on top of the fly.

50. Repeat side trimming on the other side.

48. Trim the sides of the flared deer-body hair. Trim both the white and red hair in an amount equal to the amount you trimmed off the top.

51. Trim both sides so that the fly looks fairly symmetrical.

52. To form a collar behind the trimmed deer-hair head, trim the flared butts flat across. Do not trim the hairs that extend back over the fly's body.

54. Place the scissors on an outward slant, and trim off the side ends of the flared butts of the spun deer hair.

53. A view of properly trimmed butts.

55. Repeat this process on the other side of the collar.

56. This view shows the rough, trimmed collar on the fly.

57. With a little snipping here and there, form a neat collar. This view shows the finished head, trimmed so it will dive under the surface film when retrieved.

58. Apply some head cement to the thread wraps in front of the deer hair for durability.

CHAPTER 15

The Suspender

In 1999, the Susquehanna River ran extremely low and clear because of drought. We didn't catch as many fish as we normally did, and our most successful patterns did not catch as many bass during the midday hours.

I searched desperately through my boxes for a fly pattern that would work. I knew from experience that in low, clear water, white with silver overtones was a hot color combination, and it had to be fished in the surface film. That day, a client of mine, Billy Owen, remembered that I had given him a white Crippled Minnow several years earlier when we had encountered the same conditions. He rummaged through his fly box and produced a white Crippled Minnow with a white marabou tail and silver Estaz body. That fly broke our poor catching streak.

At my fly-tying desk that night, I tied up two more. To save time on the pattern, I did not use deer-body hair for the head. Instead, I chose wool and used the Thunder Creek method of forming a head on the fly. In this method, the material is tied forward of the hook eye and pulled back to form a bullet head. I added more flash to the tail, more marabou, and made the fly more robust than the white Crippled Minnows we had used earlier in the day so that it would hang longer in one place in the water.

The Suspender is the newest of all the flies in this book. It is the only pattern I have developed that doesn't imitate something I have observed in nature. I designed it solely for the manner in which I fish it, though in my experience, white and yellow have always been good colors to use in flies. A lot of guys have asked me what it represents, and I tell them I have no idea. I don't ask those kinds of questions when the fish start eating it. This pattern has caught many species of fish, including snook, redfish, smallmouth, largemouth, trout, albacore,

stripers, pike, and a Susquehanna River muskie. I now carry a few Suspenders on all my fishing trips.

This fly is enjoyable to fish because in the clear water conditions in which it is most effective, I can see the fish attack the fly. I can watch a fish rise from the bottom and inhale the Suspender as it hangs almost motionless under the surface film.

I usually retrieve the Suspender using two different techniques. One particular way is to cast it out onto the surface, give it a 12-inch strip, then stop and let it sink slowly. The Suspender flutters as it sinks and can also be twitched during the slow sinking process. The other method is to make one to three long strips, 1 to 3 feet in length, then stop and let the fly sink slowly. Most takes come during the fly's slow descent. You can vary your retrieve depending on the fish, but always be ready for the take when you stop pulling and the head of the fly starts to bob upward and the entire fly turns.

The Suspender catches snook (shown here), smallmouth and largemouth bass, and stripers. When you strip line, the fly darts forward; when you stop, the fly bobs up in the water, moving in a way that fish find hard to resist. LEFTY KREH PHOTO

135

The head of this fly is not very durable, but if you coat it for extra durability, you sacrifice some of the buoyant qualities. One of these flies will catch four or five good fish, and then I tie on a new Suspender, because when this fly is working well, sometimes nothing else will.

The Suspender

Hook:	Size 4 Mustad 3365A, 3366, S71S SS, or Tiemco 811S
Thread:	6/0 white Uni-Thread
Tail:	Yellow over white marabou
Flash:	15 to 20 strands each of pearl and silver Flashabou mixed together
Body:	Silver extra-wide metallic Estaz
Head and collar:	White sheep fleece

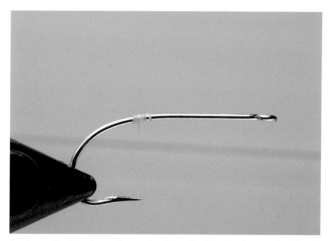

1. Attach the thread on the hook shank above the hook point.

2. Select a yellow marabou blood feather, and measure it so that it is two times the length of the hook.

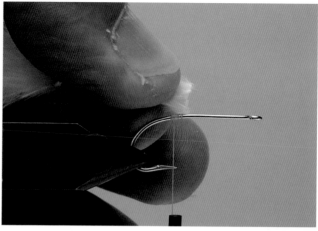

3. With a pinch wrap, tie in the butts of the marabou on top of the hook shank.

4. Wrap the thread back to a point on the shank even with the hook point. Lift up on the marabou as you wrap back over it.

5. Tie in eight to twelve strands of silver Flashabou using the fold-in method. Tie the Flashabou on top of the marabou. Cut the strands of the silver Flashabou so the longest fibers are approximately four times the hook length.

6. The proper length and position of the silver Flashabou after you trim it.

7. Tie eight to twelve strands of pearl Flashabou on top of the silver Flashabou. Cut the pearl Flashabou so that it is the same length as the silver.

8. Select a white marabou blood feather the same length as the yellow marabou feather.

9. Tie the butts of the white marabou feather on top of the Flashabou.

10. Tie in an 8-inch strand of extra-wide metallic silver Estaz on top of the white marabou blood feather. Wrap your tying thread to a point one-third the length of the hook shank behind the hook eye.

11. Wrap the Estaz forward and tie it off. Each time you make a complete wrap of Estaz around the hook shank, sweep the fibers back toward the rear of the hook with your thumb and forefinger before making another wrap.

12. Pull back the Estaz fibers as you wrap it forward, so all the fibers sweep back toward the hook bend.

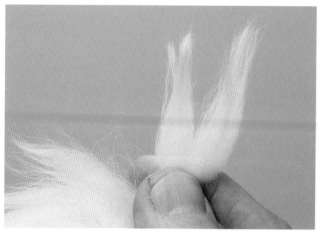

13. Select a clump of sheep fleece about the thickness of a pencil, and cut it off the skin.

14. Measure the wool so the tips extend back over half the marabou feather.

15. Make sure the thread is just behind the hook eye.

16. Hold the butts of the white wool clump so they surround the hook and the tips extend out past the hook eye. In this pattern, we tie the fibers forward and then sweep them back toward the hook bend to form a bullet head.

17. With the butts of the wool clump over the eye and against the tied-down Estaz, grasp the bundle of wool with your left thumb and forefinger. Make at least three or four turns of thread around the wool clump, ensuring that the thread stays behind the hook eye.

18. After securing the clump of wool fibers to the hook shank behind the hook eye, bind the butts of the wool clump down by wrapping the thread back to the Estaz.

19. The butts of the wool clump should be securely lashed down with thread and the bobbin positioned in front of the Estaz.

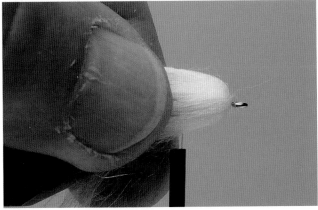

20. Pull all the tips of the wool clump back toward the bend of the hook, making sure the fibers circle the body of the fly.

21. Wrap the thread around the clump of wool, forming a bullet head.

22. Whip-finish the thread.

23. The finished fly. You can coat the thread wraps in front of the wool head with head cement for durability. Although it might make the wool head more durable, I do not coat it with anything—the fly fishes best when the wool head is left untreated.

CHAPTER 16

EZ Popper

Poppers may be one of the oldest types of flies designed for bass. For many fly anglers, they are still a favorite way to catch these fish. Poppers can be made from many types of materials. Three of the most used materials for making popping bugs in the past were cork, balsa wood, and deer-body hair. After foam was introduced to the fly-tying world, it quickly became the material of choice for poppers because it is readily available, comes in a wide range of colors, and is easy to work with and cut to shape. A wide range of closed-cell foam cylinders for making poppers are available through fly shops.

Foam cylinders come in a variety of sizes and colors. I use $^5/_{16}$-, $^3/_8$-, $^1/_2$-, and $^5/_8$-inch sizes for patterns such as the EZ Popper and Lefty's Bug. You can also use foam cylinders to form diver-type heads or sliders. All you need is a sharp razor blade or utility knife to create all the shapes you need—no sanding or grinding is necessary to shape the popper. You can shape the foam into a popper head and cup out the face if you want, though I have found that flat-faced poppers matched with the right hooks and glued on at the proper angle perform as well as cupped-out ones. Lefty's Bug and the Clouser EZ Popper do not have cupped-out faces and generate lots of disturbance during the retrieve.

When I was first introduced to foam poppers, I found that they didn't catch as many fish as cork ones. Smallmouth are attracted to noise and a partially sub-

Lefty's Bugs (left) and EZ Poppers (right) are durable, fast, and easy-to-tie poppers. I carry different color combinations for different conditions. Light colors show up in low-light conditions, and black shows up well in glare.

EZ Poppers are simple, fast, and effective poppers for everything from panfish to stripers. Saltwater EZ Poppers in chartreuse and white are good choices for surface-feeding stripers, as shown here. LEFTY KREH PHOTO

The total length of the foam body for the popper should not be any longer than two-thirds the length of the hook shank. This leaves one-third of the shank to tie the tailing materials onto. This method of measurement is reliably good on long or short shank-hooks.

If I had to pick a few colors of poppers to take along on a fishing trip, they would be white, yellow, and black. Popper color can be important at times. It usually depends on the colors of the baitfish or insects that fish are feeding on. Along weed-covered shorelines and in weed beds, poppers with green to yellow tones work best, perhaps because frogs and other foods that are the color of their surroundings are more abundant here.

Light conditions play a factor in color choice as well. Reflections from various colors change according to the angle and amount of light. Lighting has a definite effect on the way smallmouth and other species see colors. At times, for no apparent reason, smallmouth will stop hitting a white popper and their preference switches to yellow. This could be because the change in the sun's position has caused the color to look different. Dark poppers draw more strikes on a day when the sky is filled with puffy white clouds. On such days, fish may have a hard time seeing a white popper that blends in with the white clouds in the sky. On overcast or dark days, just about any color popper is effective. It may be that having the glare and reflections removed from the surface enables bass to spot prey more easily.

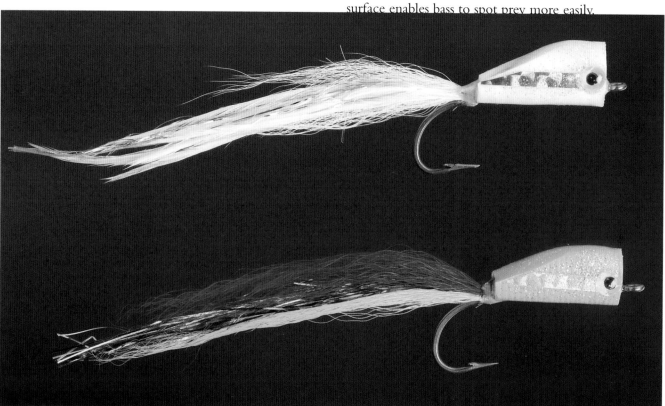

Use $1/4$-inch foam cylinders to make saltwater poppers for stripers and bluefish.

You also can reverse the EZ Popper on the hook shank to create a diver. Hook position is important. For the body to properly dive, the hook eye should protrude out of the foam head just above the foam lip. A reversed EZ Popper replicates a crippled minnow. Minnows struggling or feeding at the surface are usually quiet and don't create much disturbance. Because the diver fishes quietly, it often catches fish in low, clear water. Often a smallmouth will softly sip in the fly when the diver lies motionless on the surface. Many times I have seen large smallmouth come to investigate and sip in the fly only when all ripples have dissipated after the fly lands on the surface.

EZ Popper

Hook:	Size 2 Mustad 3365A or 34011
Thread:	Black Danville Flymaster Plus and 6/0 red Uni-Thread
Head:	1/2-inch-diameter black closed-cell foam cylinder coated with Flex Coat
Eyes:	Adhesive-back prismatic eyes, silver with black pupil
Adhesive:	Zap-A-Gap CA+
Tail:	White calf tail
Flash:	Silver Krystal Flash
Butt:	Red Estaz

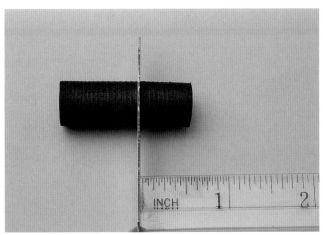

1. Cut 1/2 inch off of a 1/2-inch-wide foam cylinder with an X-Acto knife or utility knife blade.

Amberjack at Atlantic Beach, North Carolina, caught on a size 5/0 EZ Popper. JOE SCHUTE PHOTO

EZ Poppers in small sizes make great flies for panfish.
BOB CLOUSER PHOTO

2. Cut the top of the foam cylinder at a 45-degree angle.

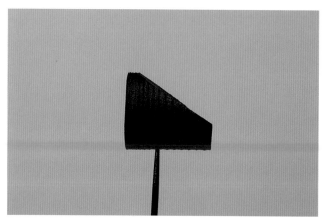

3. The cut portion should not be cut through in equal proportions. A small base and small flat platform should be left.

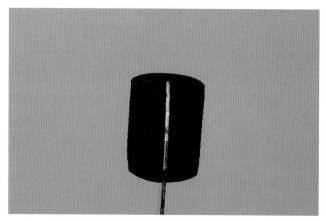

4. Turn the head upside down so the slanted portion rests on your cutting surface. Making sure the popper head is centered, cut the bottom in the center to make a slot for the hook shank.

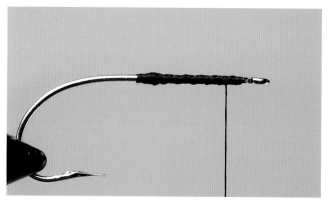

5. Attach your heavy thread at the midpoint of the hook and wrap it forward, leaving space about half a hook eye length in front of the eye. Wrap the thread back toward the hook bend with spiral wraps, forming a base to glue the body of the popper onto the hook. Repeat the screwlike wraps two to three times to ensure a solid base on which to glue the material.

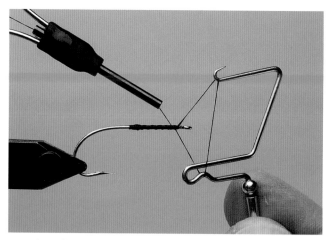

6. Whip-finish and cut the thread.

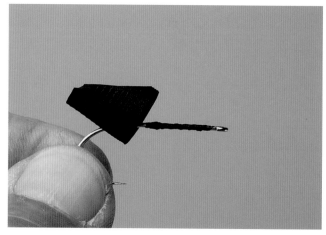

7. Push the popper body onto the hook over the bare hook shank, and slide the foam cylinder forward onto the thread wraps.

8. Position the foam cylinder on the hook so that the flat surface is well below the hook eye and the tapered end is just above level with the hook shank.

9. Line up the popper body by making sure the hook point is in line with the slot cut in the bottom of the foam popper body.

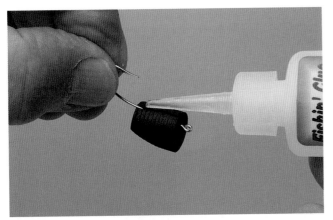

10. Run a bead of Zap-A-Gap CA+ or Fishin' Glue down the slot in the foam, covering the thread wraps on the hook shank.

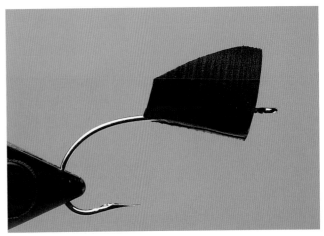

11. Before the glue dries, double-check that the foam cylinder is slanted forward on the hook shank. This positioning helps you easily lift the fly off the water on your backcast.

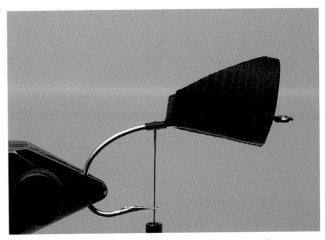

12. Attach the lighter, 6/0 thread behind the foam popper head.

13. Cut a bundle of calf-tail fibers about the thickness of half a pencil, remove the loose fibers from the base, trim the butts evenly, and measure them so they are approximately as long as the length of the hook.

14. Tie in the bundle of calf tail behind the popper head using a gathering wrap.

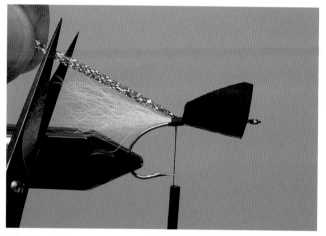

15. Tie eight to ten strands of Krystal Flash on top of the calf tail using the fold-in method.

16. Wrap the thread behind the popper body.

17. Whip-finish and cut the thread. Here is where learning how to whip-finish by hand pays off.

18. Place a prismatic stick-on eye on each side of the popper with the tip of your bodkin. Remove the popper from the vise.

19. Put a small amount of extra-fine glitter into a mixing cup. Add equal parts of Flex Coat. Thoroughly mix the glitter through the epoxy mixture.

EZ POPPER ■ 147

20. Apply Flex Coat to the entire surface of the popper body with a watercolor paint brush, spreading it evenly. Place the coated popper head on a drying wheel, and let it turn until it is dry.

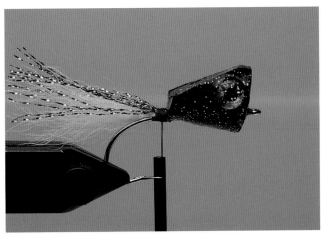

21. After the coating on the popper body has dried thoroughly, place it back into the vise.

22. Attach your tying thread behind the coated popper head, and wrap it to a point two hook eye lengths behind the head. Tie in a piece of Estaz, and wrap your tying thread to a point behind the popper head.

23. Take one and a half turns with the Estaz to the rear of the popper body and tie it off.

24. Trim the remaining Estaz.

25. Whip-finish the thread behind the popper body, and trim the thread.

26. The completed EZ Popper.

CHAPTER 17

Clouser Floating Minnow

Sometimes patterns that cause commotion on the surface, such as the EZ Popper or flat-faced hair bugs, can spook wary bass, especially in low, clear water. In these conditions, I use the Floating Minnow, a more suggestive pattern that provides a silhouette of a surface-feeding baitfish. This fly moves through water with little surface disturbance, but you can twitch it if necessary, depending on the fish's mood. Like almost all of my patterns, the Floating Minnow was developed for smallmouth bass, but it is also an excellent surface fly for saltwater species.

With its slender design, the Floating Minnow creates only a slight disturbance on the surface during a retrieve. It imitates the movements of many types of baitfish while feeding on the surface or struggling from injury. When it is at rest, the fly's foam head keeps it afloat in a semivertical position. The rear portion remains submerged during slow, tantalizing twitches of the fly. This is a trait shared by all of the most productive surface lures used by successful conventional-tackle bass fishermen. The Floating Minnow suspends nearly vertically in the surface film and triggers strikes from wary smallmouth bass.

Form the head of the Floating Minnow by gluing together two preshaped foam bodies. Wapsi distributes a product called "Foam Bug Bodies" to fly shops. These closed-cell foam bodies are available in either black or white and in several different sizes. For the Clouser Floating Minnow, purchase the spider bodies. These are the same foam bodies used to tie the foam spider with rubber legs that is so deadly for panfish, trout, and bass. In addition to keeping the fly afloat, when the foam head is positioned correctly on the hook, it makes the fly dive slightly under the surface when retrieved.

You can tie Floating Minnows in various sizes and lengths. When the combination of materials and hook and head sizes complement each other (see chart on page 151), the rear portion of the fly will be submerged while the head floats on the surface. The fly is perfectly balanced when it hangs at a 45-degree angle or near vertical in the surface film, with the forward portion of the

Though I designed the Floating Minnow for smallmouth bass, they work well anywhere predatory fish hit baitfish on the surface. Here, Lefty Kreh prepares to release a Costa Rican machaca that demolished his Floating Minnow.

BOB CLOUSER PHOTO

Use large foam bodies and reverse them for saltwater versions of the Floating Minnow (top).

Smallmouth bass slam the Floating Minnow stripped across the surface or fished dead drift with only occasional twitches. Experiment with your retrieve, depending on the fish's response to the fly. BOB CLOUSER PHOTO

and Unique Hair are also very durable when eaten by fish with sharp teeth, such as barracuda or bluefish.

Some of my favorite color combinations are chartreuse and white, tan and white, gray and white, blue and white, all black, and black over white. You can mix and match to your needs. If you want to make various color heads, color the white foam with marking pens.

You can fish the Floating Minnow in several ways. I usually fish it on a floating line, but under certain conditions, it works well fished on a medium-fast full-sinking line and a 4-foot leader. Some anglers fish it deep on fast-sinking shooting tapers. If you are using a floating line and a 9- to 12-foot leader, strip it across with occasional pauses or let it drift with the current. My favorite presentation is to give the fly a fast strip, stop and let it dead drift, make a few more fast erratic strips, and then let it dead drift again. When using a sinking line, retrieve the fly with strips interrupted by pauses. The fly rises during the pauses, imitating an injured baitfish struggling

Floating Minnows work well in different sizes and many color combinations, but my favorites are all white and chartreuse and white.

to reach safe cover on the bottom. The fish often hit when the fly starts rising.

Clouser Floating Minnow

Hook:	Size 1 Mustad 3365A, 3366, S71S SS, or Tiemco 811S
Thread:	6/0 light cahill Uni-Thread
Head:	Two white sponge rubber Foam Bug Bodies (spider, #10), coated with Flex Coat
Eyes:	Stick-on prismatic eyes
Body:	Chartreuse over white deer-tail fibers
Throat:	Red Krystal Flash
Flash:	Pearl Flashabou
Adhesive:	Zap-A-Gap CA+

EYE SIZE TO HEAD SIZE

Eye size	Head size
$3/16$ inch	4 or 6
$5/32$ inch	8
$1/8$ inch	10 or 12A

HOOK SIZE TO HEAD SIZE

Hook size	Head size
2/0	4 or 6
1/0	8
1	10
4	12A

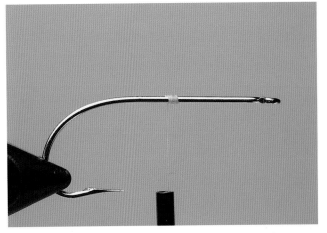

1. Attach the thread at the midpoint of the hook.

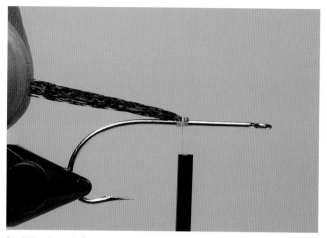

2. Tie in eight to twelve strands of red Krystal Flash, using the fold-in method. Lift up the Krystal Flash as you wrap back over the fold to secure it to the hook shank. Lifting material away from the hook shank while binding it down keeps the material on top of the hook shank.

3. Position the thread so that it is two to three thread wraps forward of the secured bundle of Krystal Flash.

4. Select a sparse clump of deer-tail fibers a quarter of the thickness of a pencil. Remove all short ends from the butts of the bundle, and measure it so that it is one and a half to two times the length of the hook.

5. Tie the deer-tail fibers on top of the hook shank in front of the Krystal Flash. Wrap the thread two to three turns in front of the secured white deer-tail fibers.

6. Tie in ten to fifteen strands of pearl Krystal Flash, using the fold-in method, and cut the long fibers about 1 inch beyond the deer-tail tips.

7. Wrap the tying thread forward a few wraps for the next step.

8. Select a sparse clump of chartreuse deer-tail fibers about the same size as the white clump, and remove the short hairs from the butt section. Trim the butts evenly.

9. Measure the chartreuse fibers so that they are as long as the white deer-tail fibers when tied in.

10. Tie the chartreuse deer hair on top of the pearl Krystal Flash. Wrap the thread forward and lift the chartreuse deer-tail fibers up at the same time.

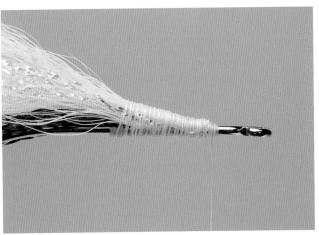

11. Form a cone with the thread, being careful not to put excessive pressure on the thread, especially when wrapping back over the previously secured and positioned materials. Apply pressure only at the forward area of the cone.

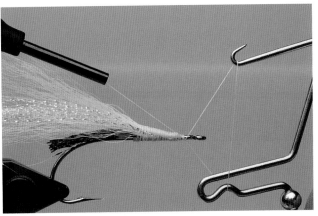

12. Whip-finish and cut the thread.

13. This is how the fly should look before gluing on the foam bodies to form a head.

14. Take the fly out of the vise, and place a drop of Zap-A-Gap CA+ on one side of the cone of thread.

17. Add a small drop of Zap-A-Gap CA+ to the hook opposite the foam body.

15. Hold a foam bug body between your thumb and forefinger, and press the hook shank with the drop of glue on it against the foam body.

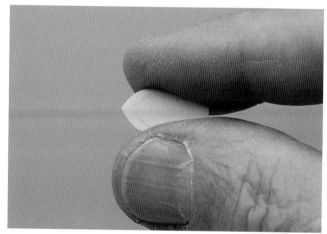

18. Hold the foam body between your thumb and forefinger.

16. Three-quarters of the body should be above the hook shank.

19. Bring the two foam body halves together by pressing the body attached to the hook against the body you are holding in your fingers. When doing this, it's important not to use too much glue; you don't want it to ooze all over the place and get on your fingers.

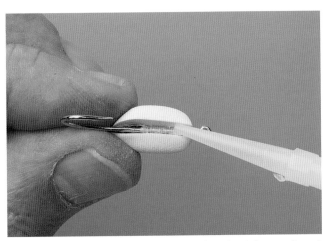

20. Holding the rear of the foam head with one hand, place a drop of glue in the slot.

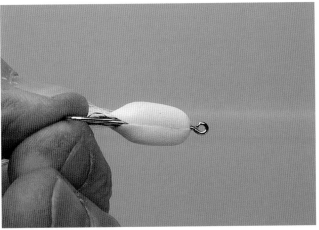

21. Lightly squeeze the two halves together. Give the glue at least two seconds to dry.

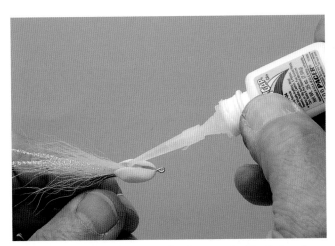

22. Repeat these steps with the top half of the foam head.

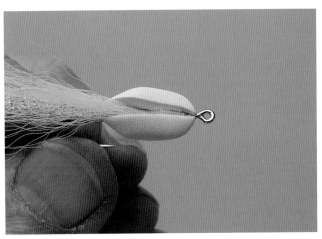

23. A little bit of Zap-A-Gap is all that is necessary for a good bond.

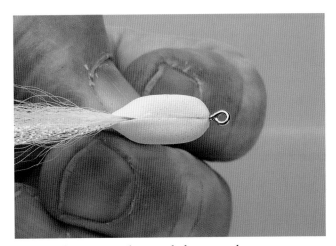

24. Gently squeeze the two halves together.

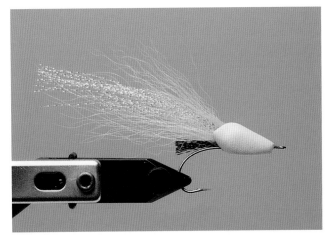

25. The two sides that form the head should be glued completely shut, and the foam should not move too much.

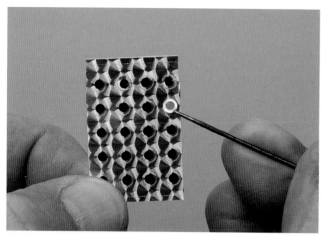

26. Remove a stick-on prismatic eye from a sheet with a bodkin.

27. Place the eye on the forward portion of the foam head. Repeat the process for the other side of the fly, making the eyes even with one another.

28. The Clouser Floating Minnow before protecting the foam head with Flex Coat.

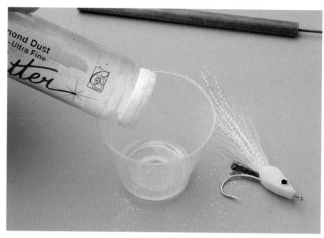

29. Put a sparse amount of extra-fine glitter into an epoxy mixing container, and add equal parts of Flex Coat. Stir the mixture until the glitter flakes and the two parts of epoxy are mixed.

30. Apply the Flex Coat with a brush to the entire foam portion of the fly. Place the fly on a rotary drier until the epoxy has cured.

31. The finished Clouser Floating Minnow.

CHAPTER 18

Bright Sides Minnow

The Bright Sides Minnow falls somewhere between the Floating Minnow and the EZ Popper. It is quieter on the surface of the water than the EZ Popper but provides more of a body profile than the Floating Minnow. I designed this fly first for salt water but now use it frequently on the Susquehanna River.

Fishing this pattern gives the illusion of a struggling, injured baitfish, with the long foam body that looks like a baitfish from below, plus the bright flash along the sides. The full length of the body lies half submerged in the surface film, which imitates some injured baitfish that struggle while lying in this position. The Bright Sides Minnow can be fished using the same techniques as the Floating Minnow.

I use metallic fish-scale Witchcraft lure tape in pink, blue, silver, gold, or chartreuse, but you can mix and match various colors and styles of the lure tape if you prefer. If you can't find it in ⅛-inch-wide strips, you can cut your own from a sheet. Match the metallic stick-on eyes to the color of the side flash. The tail fibers should match the basic color of the side flash. If you're using pink side flash, for instance, use pink fibers for the top of the tail and white for the bottom, and tie in some pink flash between the two colors of the tail. When using gold flash in the tail or on the sides, I like to use a yellow

I developed the Bright Sides Minnow to imitate wounded or crippled bait that false albacore feed on. It has become a great freshwater bass pattern as well. Here, Bob Clouser Jr. prepares to release a North Carolina false albacore that hit a Bright Sides Minnow. BOB CLOUSER PHOTO

I often fish all-white Bright Sides Minnows and just change the side flash. For fancier, color-coordinated patterns, you can match the side flash with the top color of deer tail. From top to bottom, pink, blue, and chartreuse Bright Sides Minnows.

shade, either standard or fluorescent, for the tail fibers. When adding flash in the midsection of the tail, you can use silver or pearl in the patterns or you can match the color of the side flash.

For a more durable fly with a shine to the body, I cover the completed foam portion with Flex Coat and set the fly to dry on a rotating dryer. For a sparkling effect, you can mix glitter in with the Flex Coat.

Bright Sides Minnow

Hook:	Size 1 Mustad S74S SS
Thread:	6/0 light cahill Uni-Thread
Adhesive:	Zap-A-Gap CA+
Body:	White Foam Bug Bodies (spider, #12), coated with Flex Coat
Side Flash:	1/8-inch-wide strip of gold metallic fish scale Witchcraft Lure Tape
Eyes:	3/16 inch metallic Witchcraft stick-on eyes, silver with black pupil
Tail:	Chartreuse over white deer-tail fibers
Flash:	Gold Krystal Flash

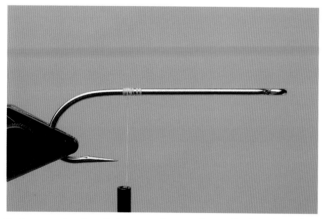

1. Insert the hook into a vise, and attach the thread to the shank above the point.

2. Select a sparse clump of white calf-tail fibers a quarter the diameter of a pencil, and cut them from the calf-tail. Remove the loose fibers from the base, and trim the butts evenly.

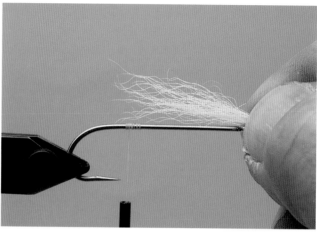

3. Measure and cut the calf-tail fibers so that they are the length of the hook shank.

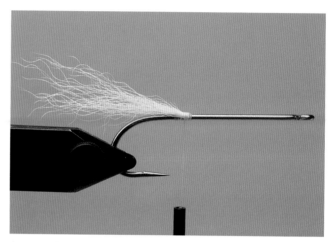

4. Tie down the butts of the calf-tail fibers onto the hook shank above the point.

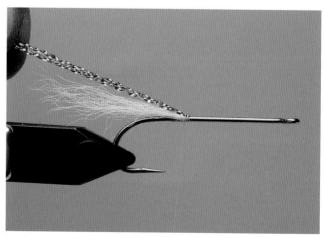

5. One wrap forward of where the calf tail is tied in, tie in eight to ten strands of Krystal Flash, using the fold-in method.

6. Trim the Krystal Flash about ¹/₄ to ¹/₂ inch longer than the calf-tail fibers.

7. Cut a sparse clump of chartreuse calf-tail hair the same thickness as the last clump of white from the skin. Remove the loose fibers from the base of the bundle, and trim the butts evenly.

8. Measure the bunch of chartreuse calf-tail fibers so that they are the same length as the white calf-tail fibers.

9. Tie the chartreuse calf-tail fibers down in front of the Krystal Flash.

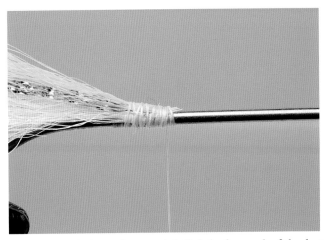

10. As you tie in each material slightly forward of the last one, the materials should remain separate. If the materials were tied directly on top of each other, you'd create a lot of bulk, which would make it difficult when you adhere the foam sides to the hook shank.

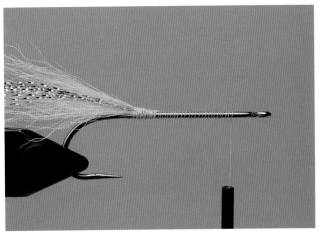

11. Spiral-wrap the thread forward to one hook eye length behind the eye.

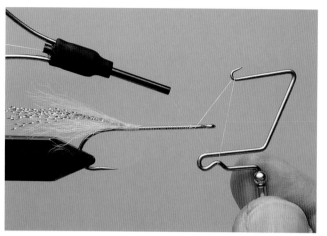

12. Whip-finish and cut the thread. Remove the hook from the vise so you can tie on the foam sides to form the body of the pattern.

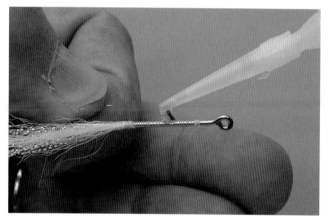

13. Place a drop of Zap-A-Gap CA+ on one side of the hook shank. Use an amount equal to or slightly less than the amount shown in the illustration.

14. Place half of a white, medium-size ant body against the side of the hook with the drop of glue on it. Position the foam so that the head is centered on the hook but the rear end is at the same level as the hook shank.

15. Side view of a properly seated foam ant body.

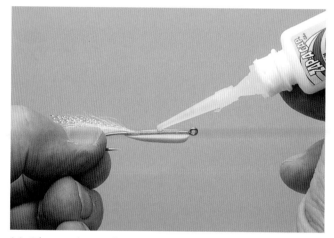

16. Place a drop of Zap-A-Gap CA+ on the hook shank opposite the foam half of the body.

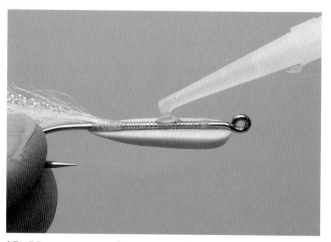

17. Use a sparse of amount of glue. You will have to hold both sides of the body together to secure both sides of the foam, and you don't want it to ooze out and get on your fingertips.

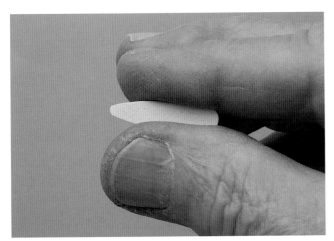

18. Place the unglued portion of the other half of the foam body between your thumb and forefinger. Place the other half of the body on top, gluing the two evenly together. Use your fingers to get both foam halves even with one another.

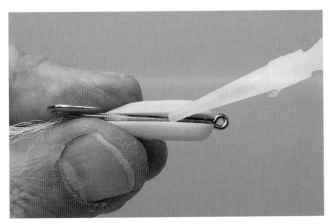

19. Squeeze a thin layer of glue on the underside of the fly where the two body halves are separated, and then squeeze the halves together. Repeat this procedure for the top of the fly.

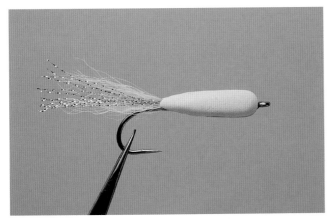

20. When you are finished gluing the sides together, they should both be level. The head should be centered on

the hook, and the rear of the foam should be in line with the hook shank. When the foam is placed this way, the tail fibers will hang in the water.

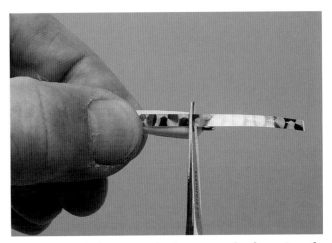

21. Cut a 45-degree angle in one end of a strip of a ¹⁄₈-inch-wide piece of reflective tape with an adhesive back. Measure the proper length of the reflective sides by holding the tape against the foam body. The tapered tip should be at the hook point, and the flat end should be about one hook eye length in front of the eye on the foam.

22. Stick the measured reflective tape on the side of the foam as in the photo. Repeat the procedure for the other side, making sure that both reflective strips are level with each other.

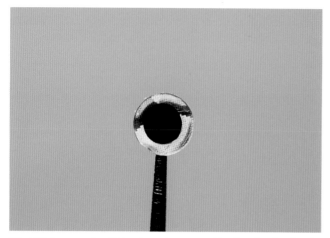

23. With your bodkin tip, select an adhesive-backed prismatic eye.

25. Coat the entire foam body with Flex Coat. Mix extrafine glitter into the epoxy if you like. Set the fly on a rotating dryer overnight.

24. Place an eye on each side so that the outer curve of the eye (nearest the hook eye) just covers the cut portion of the reflective strip.

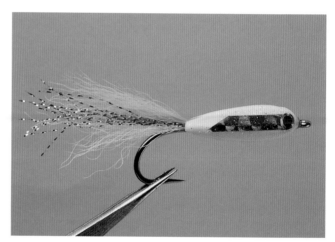

26. The finished Bright Sides Minnow.

CHAPTER 19

Clouser Drake

Mayflies are important insects in fly fishing. Most freshwater species depend on them for food at some stage of their lives. Many species and various sizes of mayflies live where I fish in Pennsylvania, but I love the large mayflies, such as the green and brown drakes and the massive hatches of whiteflies on the Susquehanna and Yellow Breeches. I like these hatches because I prefer fishing large dry flies. Not only are they easier for me to see, but they also attract larger fish. Some of the coldwater trout streams I fish in Pennsylvania have yearly hatches of these large mayflies. They are abundant in some sections of these coldwater fisheries and can also be found on the Susquehanna River. The central section of the river near Middletown gets an emergence of brown drakes during the last few weeks of July and throughout August. They start emerging at dusk and continue for a few hours after dark. At this time, smallmouth selectively rise to these large insects and single them out from other mayflies hatching during the same time period.

To trick these smallmouth, I went to my fly-tying desk and looked at a number of fly patterns I could copy. Many of the large patterns did not float well, even with floatant. I had also noticed that the naturals' legs supported their bodies and kept them above the water's surface, and their tails did not touch the surface either. With traditional patterns, the bodies would not remain above the surface film; the abdomens and tails touched the water's surface, distorting the fly's silhouette.

So I created the Clouser Drake, which has the proper silhouette and rides high on the water. The heavy hackle from one end to the other was inspired by the effectiveness of one of my favorite trout flies, the Bivisible. The high wing makes the fly easy to see and helps balance it when it lands on the water. To also help balance the fly, I use long, dark, blackish brown moose body-hair fibers tilted upward for the tail. All the natural drakes I have observed drift on the water's surface without their tails or abdomens touching the water. I cut a V-shape out of the bottom of the hackle fibers so the fly will land on the surface upright. Trimming the bottom of the hackle helps the fly sit on the surface like the natural on almost every cast.

Lefty Kreh lifts a ball of Whiteflies (Ephoron leukon) *during a heavy hatch on the Susquehanna River. The Clouser Drake with white or cream hackles and the White Wulff are high-riding, easy-to-see imitations for whiteflies.*
BOB CLOUSER PHOTO

163

The Clouser Drake works well for trout on streams with hatches of whiteflies and brown, green, and yellow drakes.
BOB CLOUSER PHOTO

My first chance to try this new pattern was on one of Pennsylvania's largest limestone creeks, Penns Creek, during the green drake hatch in early June. It consistently caught large trout better than any other pattern I had in tried in my twenty years of fishing that creek. I could not wait until I could test it on the smallmouth in late July on the Susquehanna.

The brown drakes begin to emerge the last week of July. I anchored the boat near a small pool lined with rock ledges and waited for them to appear. The whitefly hatch was already in full swing, and smallmouth were taking the naturals. My theory was that the larger bass would single out the larger brown drake naturals, and I sat through all this feeding activity to see if I was right. As soon as the first drake appeared, it drifted like a giant among the hundreds of smaller whiteflies. Suddenly a small, subtle ring appeared on the surface as the drake vanished. I could tell the fish was a larger bass by the rise. I cast my new fly to a spot three feet above the riseform. The imitation slowly drifted along the current seam and was sucked in by the smallmouth. When the fish went airborne, its 18-inch-long body glistened in the fading light. The Clouser Drake has since become my generic pattern for all large mayflies; I just change the size and color to match the naturals.

Properly dressed with dry-fly floatant, these large imitations sit high on the surface. Conventional trout patterns that imitate a lot of insects that bass feed on in the Susquehanna River do not float very well. The film in many warmwater rivers like this one contains a lot of dirt. A traditionally dressed dry fly has a life span of just a couple casts in this type of water, even when treated with floatant. But this heavily hackled fly with its large deer-hair wing floats like a cork when treated with floatant. Another advantage of these large drake imitations is that they can be seen easily in the fading light at dusk.

Regardless of what is hatching, these big flies will catch bass because fish are used to seeing large naturals all summer long. This is also true on trout streams, such as Penns Creek or the upper Delaware River. Once the big flies start hatching, it's a good idea to fish a large dry fly, because the fish seem to key on the large insects. Even when the small mayflies are hatching, the bass take the larger flies, so why bother with the small stuff? The Clouser Drake's big, meaty form and wing silhouette draw bass and trout to this fly.

Clouser Green Drake Dun

Hook:	Size 10 Mustad 94831
Thread:	6/0 light cahill Uni-Thread
Tail:	Dark brownish black moose body-hair fibers
Body:	Pale yellow rabbit dubbing
Wing:	Dark natural brown deer-body hair from back of deer
Hackle:	Dry-fly-quality saddle hackles: light ginger (rear hackle), grizzly, and ginger (front)

Clouser Brown Drake

Hook:	Size 10 Mustad 94831
Thread:	6/0 light cahill Uni-Thread
Tails:	Three moose body-hair fibers
Body:	Rusty brown rabbit fur
Hackle:	Dry-fly-quality saddle hackles. Brown (rear) and grizzly and brown (front)
Wing:	natural dark deer-body hair from back of deer

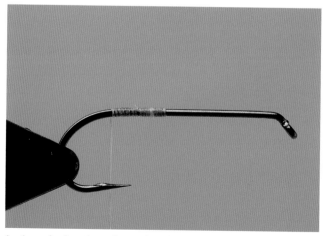

1. Attach the thread on the shank above the hook point and position it above the barb.

2. Apply a light amount of dubbing wax to the inside tip of your forefinger. Apply only enough wax to make your forefinger tip tacky.

3. Place a small amount of pale yellow Superfine synthetic dubbing on your forefinger, and dub it onto the thread by rubbing your thumb across the dubbing and thread. When applying dubbing in this manner, always squeeze and push your thumb away from you—in one direction, never back and forth.

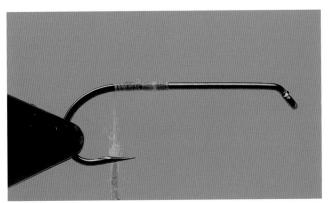

4. Continue applying sparse amounts of dubbing until you have built up about ¹/₂ inch of dubbing on the thread.

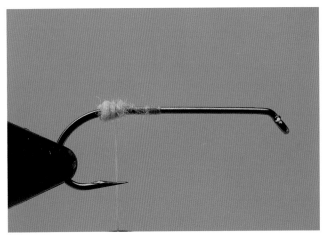

5. Wrap the dubbing around the hook shank at the point above the barb, forming a small bump.

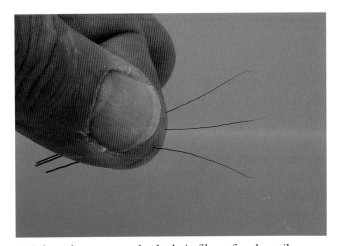

6. Select three moose body-hair fibers for the tail.

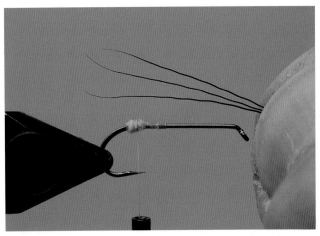

7. Measure the tailing fibers for length so that they are approximately one to one and a quarter times the length of the hook.

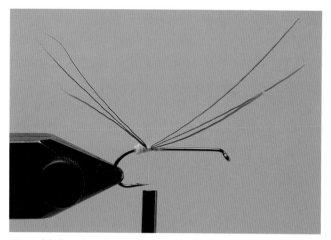

8. Hold the three moose-body fibers on top of the hook shank in front of the dubbing bump. Gently wrap the thread over the moose fibers and around the hook shank. Wrap the thread toward the bump of dubbing, forcing the moose fibers to rise.

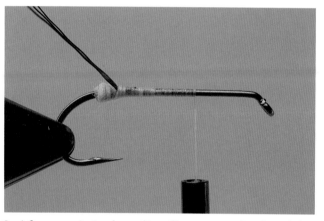

9. After you tie in the tailing fibers, wrap the thread forward to a point one-third the shank length in front of the hook eye.

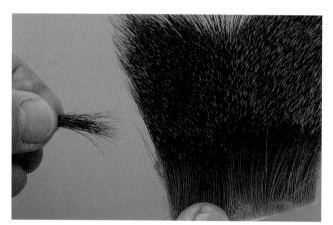

10. Cut a bundle of deer-body hair about half the thickness of a pencil. When selecting deer hair for a wing, use the dark mottled hair that usually comes from the back

portion of the body. Pull out any loose fibers from the bottom of the bundle, and trim the butts evenly.

11. Measure the deer-hair bundle so that it is one and a half times the length of the hook, from eye to hook bend.

12. Hold the bundle of deer hair against the hook, with the tips facing forward. Make two loose gathering wraps with the thread around the bundle and hook shank, and slowly lift as you apply pressure to set the fibers in place. Wrap the thread back to secure the butts of the deer-hair bundle to the hook shank.

13. Lift the remaining deer-hair butts, and cut them off at an angle using a sharp pair of scissors.

14. Cover the butts completely with the thread, forming a buoyant underbody for the fly. Wrap the tying thread to a position on the hook shank directly above the point.

15. Select a dry-fly-quality ginger saddle hackle for a size 10 hook. To size a hackle, bend it around the hook shank and pull the hackle up, causing the barbules to extend down toward the hook point. If the barbules extend past the hook point at least a quarter to half the width of the hook gap, you have the correct size.

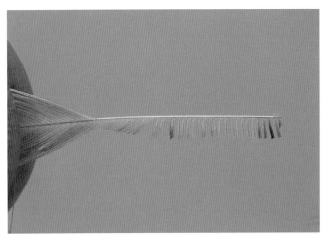

16. Prepare the ginger saddle hackle for tying in by removing the barbules from one side of the hackle stem butt. Cut off the barbules on the opposite side of the saddle hackle stem with scissors as in the photo.

17. Place the hackle stem against the side of the hook, and secure it with the thread by wrapping forward half the distance between the rear of the deer-hair clump and the tie-in point of the saddle hackle stem.

18. Fold the hackle stem back, and wrap the thread over the doubled-back stem.

19. As you wrap back over the doubled-back stem, position the thread so that your first wrap of dubbing touches the dubbing ball.

20. Apply approximately 2 to 2¹/₂ inches of pale yellow Superfine dubbing to the thread. The dubbing rope should have an increasingly thick taper as you dub down the thread.

21. You need enough dubbing for the entire body of the fly, but do not put too much on to start. It's much easier to add dubbing than it is to take it away.

22. Wrap the dubbing forward to a position behind the wing of deer-body hair, building a smoothly tapered body.

23. Move the thread in front of the wing, and then wrap the thread back against the front of the wing until it flares upward.

24. Take four to five turns with the thread around the base of the wing, and then wrap the thread behind the wing and form a bed of thread for the saddle hackle.

25. Attach a pair of hackle pliers to the tip section of the ginger saddle hackle, and twist the saddle hackle to the right, making five turns. Spiral-wrap the hackle forward, stopping at the back of the bed of thread and not wrapping all the way to the wing.

26. Twisting the saddle hackle before wrapping it helps the fibers flare as you palmer the hackle through the body.

27. Tie off the saddle hackle at the beginning of the bed of thread.

28. Make sure there is ample room on the bed of thread behind the wing clump after tying down the ginger saddle hackle.

30. Prepare a ginger saddle hackle in the same manner, and tie it down directly over the grizzly saddle hackle.

29. Prepare ¹/₄ inch of a grizzly saddle hackle by stripping one side of the hackle stem and cutting the barbules very short on the other. Place the hackle stem on the near side of the thread bed, and tie it in place.

31. Bind down the stems of both saddle hackles, making even turns of the thread behind and in front of the wing. Make sure you leave one full eye length of bare hook shank in front of the tied-in saddle hackle stems.

32. Wrap the thread back against the wing.

33. Twist a ¹/₂-inch length of pale yellow Superfine dubbing onto the thread, and wrap it in front of the wing.

34. Attach the hackle pliers to the tip of the ginger saddle hackle, and make five right-hand twists in the hackle. Wrap the hackle four turns behind the wing and three turns in front of the wing. Tie it off one eye length behind the hook eye, and cut the remaining ginger hackle tip as close to the tie-in point as possible.

35. Attach the hackle pliers to the tip of the grizzly saddle hackle, and spiral-wrap it through the ginger hackle barbules. Tie off the grizzly saddle hackle one eye length behind the eye of the hook, and cut the feather as close to the tie-in point as possible.

36. Form a neat head with the thread. If you have stray fibers leaning forward, sweep them back with one hand as you wrap over the base of them with the other.

37. Whip-finish and snip the thread.

38. Spread the wing by gently pulling the fibers apart, in line with the hook shank.

39. Finished Green Drake Dun. To imitate the female egg-depositing spinner, change the color of the ginger saddle hackle in front of and behind the wing to a brown saddle hackle. Add a little bit of cement to the thread for more durability. When using cement on dry flies, be careful not to get any of it on the materials or have it soak up into the body of the fly. Trim the hackles on the bottom of the fly flat so the Drake always lands upright after you cast and rides low on the water.

INDEX